Consider the Lilies

Consider the Lilies

A GIRL'S QUIET TIME WITH THE FATHER

TERESA NUCKOLS

Illustrated by Rosemary Nuckols

Lilac Meadows Publishing

Published by Lilac Meadows Publishing
www.lilacmeadows.com

ISBN: 978-0-9816328-0-3

Illustrations by Rosemary Nuckols

Cover Design by Daniel Nuckols, Highlands Graphics,
www.highlandsgraphics.com

Picture on cover by Daniel Nuckols featuring: Angela Rose Nuckols.

Printed by White Birch Printing
501 W. Beaver Brook Ave.
Spooner, WI 54801
715.635.8147

THIS BOOK IS LOVINGLY DEDICATED TO

My Heavenly Father:
Who has given me salvation through His Son, the Lord Jesus
Christ, so that I may come to Him without fear or guilt having
been cleansed from all sin by Christ's precious blood, being
made fit to enjoy God's presence because of His provision.

*Blessed be the God and Father of our Lord Jesus Christ,
who has blessed us in Christ with every spiritual blessing in
the heavenly places, even as He chose us in Him before the
foundation of the world, that we should be holy and blameless before Him. In love He predestined us for adoption as
sons through Jesus Christ, according to the purpose of His
will, to the praise of His glorious grace, with which He has
blessed us in the Beloved.* Ephesians 1:3-6.

My Mom:
Whose selfless love and availability to just sit and talk has
meant more than words can ever say. My mom is my best
friend, and I long to follow in her example of godly woman-
hood. She has laid down her life for each of her children
that we may seek to know the Lord and enjoy His presence.

The children of Your servants will live in Your presence...
Psalm 102:28. NIV

My Dad:
Who has displayed the Father's love and mercy to me. His
steadfast commitment to please God, no matter what others
may think, has been a wonderful example. I am pleased to
be called his daughter.

...The glory of children is their fathers. Proverbs 17:6.

A Special Thank You to:

~ Dad, for his practical help and insight about all that goes into publishing a book.

~ Mom, whose encouragement helped keep me going when I otherwise would have given up. Her beautiful gift for art has added a very special touch to this book.

~ My brother, Dan, for his excellent work in designing the book cover.

~ My sister, Angela, for being willing to pose for the sweet picture that appears on the cover of this book.

~ My brothers, Luke and Josh, who graciously kept me company during the many hours of typing, editing, and revising this book while in Dad's office.

~ My sister, Melissa and her husband, Josh, for their encouragement and prayers while I was working on this book.

~ My wonderful fiancé, Zachery Ender, whose love and prayers have been a beautiful gift and wonderful source of encouragement from the Lord during this season of my life. I've greatly appreciated his Biblical insights and his practical advice for the book writing process.

~ My grandpa, who lovingly took great interest in my writing endeavors from the start. He gave such kind encouragement, generous support, and faithfully prayed for me throughout the whole process.

~ Linda Ferraro, for her encouragement and expertise as she proofed my manuscripts. The Lord answered my prayers by sending Linda to help me through that seemingly overwhelming process.

~ All of my loving family and friends, whose prayers, encouragement, and interest in this book greatly blessed me, and inspired me to keep writing.

Thank you from the bottom of my heart!

TABLE OF CONTENTS

A Letter from My Heart

Dear Sisters,

As I write this book, I want to share with you a message from my heart. Sometimes I do not know how to really describe the joy I have felt during times of undisturbed moments in the Lord's presence. It is a very personal, solitary thing, but how I wish that others could experience the same closeness and inspiration from being in the Lord's presence that I have begun to know! I cannot force others to desire or understand this; I can only point the way, and then show how beautiful Jesus is so that they will desire nothing other than to seek His presence.

Walking closely with the Lord isn't always a "bed of roses." It is not easy or "fun" as the world would think, but it is worth it! Life has its ups and downs, but the Lord's sustaining presence makes all the difference. Yet, if you do not know the Lord Jesus as your Savior, you will not be able to enter into His holy presence.

We can't come before this Holy One on our terms. God requires repentance and faith. As sinners we need to be covered by Christ's blood and be wearing His robe of righteousness. None of us have ever kept God's perfect law. As a result we are condemned to an eternal separation from Him – a place called hell. Can our works atone for our sin? No! Only the saving blood of Christ, the Perfect One.

We cannot trust Christ for salvation while still holding onto our sins. That would be impossible, since it would mean going in two different directions. When we see our awful state of sinful helplessness and turn to Jesus for merciful redemption, we must turn 180 degrees, as we acknowledge our condition to the Lord.

> "Repentance is to leave
> The sins we loved before,
> And show that we in earnest grieve,
> By doing so no more."[1]

Cry out to Him for His forgiveness and salvation, and then have faith that God hears your prayer and that He will save you.

> *If you confess with your mouth that Jesus is Lord and believe in your heart that God raised Him from the dead, you will be saved. For with the heart one believes and is justified, and with the mouth one confesses and is saved.* Romans 10:9-10.

Having the blessed assurance that we are saved is offered to us when we call on the Lord's name for salvation.

> *I write these things to you who believe in the name of the Son of God that you may know that you have eternal life.* I John 5:13.

Many of you who read this I'm sure already know this sweet Savior and are longing to grow in your walk with Him. It is my prayer that this book would be an encouragement to you, no matter what age you are, regardless of the past you've had, and despite the difficulties you will face.

It is my desire to share with you lessons that I have learned from the Father and His Word, not setting myself up as a pattern to copy, but to inspire you to seek the Lord for yourself as you are guided by the Holy Spirit. I am not sufficient for this task in myself, but only in God who alone makes me a competent minister of His new covenant.

> *Such is the confidence that we have through Christ toward God. Not that we are sufficient in ourselves to claim anything as coming from us, but our sufficiency is from God, who has made us competent to be ministers of a new covenant, not of the letter but of the Spirit. For the letter kills, but the Spirit gives life.* II Corinthians 3:4-6.

I encourage you to embrace godly femininity as a sweet gift from the Lord. He created women with a longing for beauty and to be beautiful – in themselves and their world around them. Our heavenly Designer knows that and wants us to come to Him, trusting that God will provide beautiful raiment for our hearts, souls, and bodies, as we offer our lives to Him. As you come surrendered into Jesus' presence each day, you will be molded into His beautiful image. This will result in bringing beauty to your little realm of influence that He placed you in.

> *And let the beauty of the LORD our God be upon us:*
> *and establish thou the work of our hands upon us;*
> *yea, the work of our hands establish thou it.*
> Psalm 90:17. KJV

So, dear sisters, I invite you to come with me and "consider the lilies," and in so doing get a better glimpse of our Father's loving care for His precious daughters. He is waiting to meet with you. Will you come?

Matthew 6:25-34

Therefore I tell you, do not be anxious about your life, what you will eat or what you will drink, nor about your body, what you will put on. Is not life more than food, and the body more than clothing? Look at the birds of the air: they neither sow nor reap nor gather into barns, and yet your heavenly Father feeds them. Are you not of more value than they? And which of you by being anxious can add a single hour to his span of life? And why are you anxious about clothing? **Consider the lilies of the field, how they grow: they neither toil nor spin, yet I tell you, even Solomon in all his glory was not arrayed like one of these. But if God so clothes the grass of the field, which today is alive and tomorrow is thrown into the oven, will he not much more clothe you, O you of little faith?** *Therefore do not be anxious, saying, "What shall we eat?" or "What shall we drink?" or "What shall we wear?" For the Gentiles seek after all these things, and your heavenly Father knows that you need them all. But seek first the kingdom of God and His righteousness, and all these things will be added to you. Therefore do not be anxious about tomorrow, for tomorrow will be anxious for itself. Sufficient for the day is its own trouble.*

Chapter 1

Come to the Garden

Come Away with Me

By Anne Fuller

"Come away with me," my Beloved calleth.
To the vineyards we will go, walking hand in hand.
And who is this that would call me to follow?
He is my King and my Lord; He is my dearest friend.
I will go when He calls unto me.

There was once a time when fear kept me from following
For the shadows were dark and I could not see.
Then came my Lord to me; He opened mine eyes to Calvary.
And I fell in love with Him who had died for me.

And who is this who would call me to follow?
He is my King and my Lord. He is my dearest friend.
I will go when He calls unto me. My beloved one calls.
I will go for He is calling unto me.[2]

In the dewy stillness, as the first rays of dawn streak across the sky, all of the flowers are decked with dewdrops like a dazzling string of costly pearls. Instead of being pearly white, the beads on their necklace are iridescent and translucent, reflecting all of the colorful flowers around and capturing their perfect likeness in the liquid heart of each little droplet of water. The roses are elegant and romantic, as they give off a spicy, sweet fragrance in the fresh morning air. The poppies are bright and cheerful. The black-eyed-susans and daisies lift their sunny faces, ready to catch the first sunbeam. At a closer glance, the garden flowers are each an intricate science study in and of themselves. The delicate petals, leaves, and stems of each one are unique, yet similar. Their colors include almost every hue and shade known to man; their fragrance varies from sweet to spicy, subtle to flashy. Wildflowers are some of my favorites, but there is nothing like a well laid-out garden, that is expertly planned, planted, watered, and cared for. For many centuries, gardens have brightened up many little corners of this earth, as some beautiful souls have been inspired to "bloom where they are planted."

Have you ever taken time to really look at a flower ~ noticing all the intricate parts, the number of petals, the subtle fragrance, the variety and shades of colors?

Jesus charged His followers to "consider the lilies." There is something wonderful about considering (i.e. studying, pondering, examining, contemplating) the amazing intricacy of God's creation – specifically the flower – that causes us to get a clearer picture of His character and the care He gives to His creation.

> *For what can be known about God is plain to them, because God has shown it to them. For His invisible attributes, namely His eternal power and divine nature, have been clearly perceived, ever since the creation of the world, in the things that have been made. So they are without excuse.* Romans 1:19-20.

Unbelievers are without an excuse since they can clearly see God's divine nature displayed in creation. How much more should God's children be in tune to considering and learning more about His creation, so that they may know and glorify God!

It should be no surprise that most of the famous scientists through the years were Christians. From their Biblical worldview they had a better understanding of the world around them.

The vast attributes of God are displayed in His creation. The magnificent mountains show His majesty. The powerful, stormy winds cause us to tremble at God's might. The soft, fragrant spring breezes can make us contemplate His gentleness. The breath-taking beauty of an evening sunset reminds us of how glorious He is.

When you are weary and long to rest in Jesus' presence, come to the garden and consider how God will care for you, much more than He cares for the beautiful, intricately made lilies. Flowers, unlike people, will not live forever. If God graciously clothes and provides for the temporary grass of the field, how much more will He care for eternal human souls?

> *And why are you anxious about clothing? Consider the lilies of the field, how they grow: they neither toil nor spin, yet I tell you, even Solomon in all his glory was not arrayed like one of these. But if God so clothes the grass of the field, which today is alive and tomorrow is thrown into the oven, will He not much more clothe you, O you of little faith?* Matthew 6:28-30.

God clothes flowers of the field like Solomon. My grandpa has commented that Solomon must have been a "snappy-dresser!" Let us grow in our faith and trust in God for who He is and for what He can do.

Christ's Invitation

I love that precious invitation of Christ's - **"Come."** He gently says to the sin-weary world:

> **Come** *to Me, all who labor and are heavy laden, and I will give you rest."* Matthew 11:28.

He calls to the disciples:

> **Come***, follow Me and I will make you fishers of men."* Matthew 4:19. NIV

> *Jesus said, "Let the little children* **come** *to Me and do not hinder them, for to such belongs the kingdom of heaven."* Matthew 19:14.

In the Old Testament the Lord invited the children of Israel to come before Him in repentance so that they may receive His redemption.

> **Come** *now, let us reason together, says the Lord: though your sins are like scarlet, they shall be as white as snow; though they are red like crimson, they shall become like wool. If you are willing and obedient, you shall eat the good of the land; but if you refuse and rebel, you shall be eaten by the sword…*
> Isaiah 1:18-20.

In the last book of the Bible, we find this beautiful invitation emphasized and repeated again, this time given by the Spirit and Christ's glorious bride, the church. We, the hearers, are exhorted to spread this invitation as well, telling others to come to this wonderful Savior that we know.

> *The Spirit and the Bride say,* **"Come."** *And let the one who hears say,* **"Come."** *And let the one who is thirsty* **come***; let the one who desires take the water of life without price.* Revelation 22:17

I don't think that there is any word of invitation like this simple little word – **come**. We hear our parents tell us when to come home, we hear our mother telling us to come to supper, we rejoice when we are invited to come to a birthday party or a wedding. Yet, all of these pale in comparison with being invited to come into the Lord's presence.

Christ's invitation to come to Him entails leaving our tasks, our burdens, our weariness at His feet and then resting in His presence, allowing Him to make us what He wants us to be. It requires leaving the world behind, dying to self, coming to the Judge as we are and hearing Him pronounce the guilty free because of the blood of Jesus His Son.

We are invited to come to Jesus, come to the garden to consider the lilies, and then to come follow Him.

> "I come to the garden alone,
> While the dew is still on the roses;
> And the voice I hear, falling on my ear;
> The Son of God discloses.
> And He walks with me, and He talks with me,
> And He tells me I am His own,
> And the joy we share as we tarry there,
> None other has ever known."[3]

During my teen years I went through a really difficult season, often called "depression." I struggled greatly with viewing my Christian walk as a performance, trying so hard to please the Lord and do everything right to gain His acceptance and approval. Praise the Lord that He showed me His truth through the wise counsel of my parents, through good Christian books, and most importantly through His own Word and Spirit, "that Christ had paid it all."

When the Lord delivered me from my depression and was teaching me of my position in Christ, I found it so helpful to spend a lot of time alone with Him, especially out in His creation. At our home in the suburbs where my family and I lived at that time, I often would go out and sit by our garden to read God's Word and pray. I had some really special times communing there with Jesus as I looked up into the blue sky with fluffy white clouds. The heavens really do "declare the glory of God!" Psalm 19:1.

During that sweet time of seeking the Lord and growing in Him, I rarely kept track of time. I came to Him and His Word so thirsty, and I wouldn't leave until I was filled to overflowing. It was a unique season of life, unlike any other I've known before or since.

I often found myself singing my Grandma Ruthie's favorite hymn, "In the Garden." My heart could echo every line of that hymn. I was learning firsthand the importance of taking time each day to spend with Jesus.

It is not necessary to have an actual garden to go to for our quiet-times, but there is something so uplifting about being out in God's creation as we seek His face. Where did Jesus go in the agony of His soul as He sought to do His father's will? To the Garden of Gethsemane.

The point is not where you go, but Who you are with. Seek Jesus, wherever you are. He invites you to come into His presence to give you rest and to equip you for service. He is the Great Vinedresser and Gardener, so allow your gentle Savior to prune away any and everything in your life that is not pleasing to Him, so that you may become more fruitful.

> *"I am the true vine, and My Father is the vinedresser. Every branch in Me that does not bear fruit He takes away, and every branch that does bear fruit He prunes, that it may bear more fruit."* John 15:1-2.

LISTENING TO CHRIST'S VOICE

In the stillness of His creation we can hear the Lord's gentle voice speaking to our hearts through His Word, as we see His character displayed in what He has made.

> "He speaks, and the sound of His voice,
> Is so sweet the birds hush their singing,

And the melody that He gave to me
Within my heart is ringing.
And He walks with me, and He talks with me,
And He tells me I am His own;
And the joy we share as we tarry there,
None other has ever known."[4]

This blessed communion gives us a reason to rejoice and sing for joy. The Lord will restore our fruitfulness and renew our strength, as we come to our "garden" to seek His face. Our thirsty souls will be satisfied with His goodness.

Hear the word of the Lord, O nations, and declare it in the coastlands far away; say, 'He who scattered Israel will gather him, and will keep him as a shepherd keeps his flock.' For the Lord has ransomed Jacob and has redeemed him from hands too strong for him. They shall come and sing aloud in the height of Zion, and they shall be radiant over the goodness of the Lord, over the grain, the wine, and the oil, and over the young of the flock and the herd; their life shall be like a watered garden, and they shall languish no more. Then shall the young women rejoice in the dance, and the young men and the old shall be merry. I will turn their mourning into joy; I will comfort them, and give them gladness for sorrow. I will feast the soul of the priests with abundance, and My people shall be satisfied with My goodness, declares the Lord. Jeremiah 31:10-14.

I have sometimes wished that I could spend my lifetime in the garden with the Lord, but He has work for me to do and a cross for me to bear.

*Then Jesus told His disciples, "If anyone would **come** after Me, let him deny himself and take up his cross and follow Me."* Matthew 16:24.

Following Jesus is not always easy according to the world's standards. It requires denying self and a complete surrender of our will, though it certainly is worth it!

"I'd stay in the garden with Him
Though the night around me be falling;
But He bids me go, thru voice of woe,
His voice to me is calling.
And He walks with me, and He talks with me,
And He tells me I am His own;
And the joy we share as we tarry there
None other has ever known."[5]

Though there may be trials, or unpleasant tasks along the way, we can cling to the wonderful promise that Jesus will never leave us. He will walk with us and talk with us as we do our mundane tasks, as well as in our quiet places of seeking Him.

In the trials that the Lord brings us through in this life, the Lord is really molding us into His image. He longs for us to seek Him with a deep desire and passion to know Him and to become holy like He is. All of the sweat and tears shed in plowing and preparing our lives as His Word is being planted and cultivated in our heart, will someday result in beautiful blossoms and fruit for our King – the gentle Gardener.

My grandpa often likes to tell me, since he heard the title of this book, "Go consider the lilies now!" Are we willing to take time to consider the lilies, and learn to trust the loving care of our Father?

He takes great delight in His children, so don't be afraid to come to Him just as you are.

CHAPTER 2

The Delighted Gardener

JUST AS I AM
By Charlotte Elliott

Just as I am, without one plea,
But that Thy blood was shed for me,
And that Thou bidst me come to Thee,
O Lamb of God, I come, I come.

Just as I am, and waiting not
To rid my soul of one dark blot,
To Thee whose blood can cleanse each spot,
O Lamb of God, I come, I come.

Just as I am, though tossed about
With many a conflict, many a doubt,
Fightings and fears within, without,
O Lamb of God, I come, I come.

Just as I am, poor, wretched, blind;
Sight, riches, healing of the mind,
Yea, all I need in Thee to find,
O Lamb of God, I come, I come.

Just as I am, Thou wilt receive,
Wilt welcome, pardon, cleanse, relieve;
Because Thy promise I believe,
O Lamb of God, I come, I come.

*Softly the Master Gardener treads across the dew-soaked
lawn to his little bower of greenery and flowering blooms. The
misty morning is still fresh and new before the heat of the hot
summer sun starts beating upon his weary back.*

*With a trowel in hand, the big, gentle man stoops to begin the
work that has become his lifetime labor of love, planting and
caring for his own dear flowers.*

*The birds are singing, the dew drops sparkle, as the
Gardener revels in the sights and sounds of his haven. He even
enjoys the smell of the rich soil that cakes his work-worn hands,
filling each crack and crevice, including his chipped fingernails.
He doesn't mind the dirt a bit, for it is a sign of his labor, a part
of his garden – real nutrients that will make his garden grow.*

*When his work is done for the day, he sits back and admires
his array of floral treasures. Ruby-red roses, amethyst colored
asters, sunny-gold coreopsis, pearly pink carnations, satiny-
white lilies, and fragrant magenta phlox. Despite all of the
showy beauty of these dazzling blooms, the shy violets have
always been his favorite. Their little dew-drop faces reflect his
own spirit of gentle shyness and modesty. Their timidity evokes
a deep fondness in his heart for the modest little blossoms
above all the other flowers in his garden. The Gardener is
amused by their funny antics as they spontaneously pop up in
hopeful expectation everywhere, even where they weren't originally planted. Yet, he feels as if the violets will never really
know or bask in his care and delight as the other flowers seem
to do. Exactly why, he is not sure.*

*The shy violets just don't understand the Gardener's favoring
fondness for them, for they always seem to hold back from his
gentle presence, fearing his disapproval. They don't realize that
the Gardener likes them just as they are, desiring them to grow
healthy and strong.*

I wonder if some of us are like the shy violets, hiding from
our dear Master Gardener's work in our lives and fearing His
disapproval.

Several years ago, on a sunny September afternoon, and I

was home from Bible School for the day. As I was sitting by our deep chestnut colored piano, desiring to seek the Lord's presence, I realized I was holding back, afraid to come to Him as I was. I contemplated that thought, wondering why it was so.

Out of self-centered timidity we often look at ourselves and our unworthiness. Maybe we even are trying to fix ourselves up to be "presentable" to the Lord, when all we need to do is come to Him, just as we are, trusting Him to fix our problems, cleanse our sins, and patch up our mistakes.

Often I have felt as a Christian that I always need to change, becoming better and better. Many times I realize all too well the imperfections of my soul. Such peace comes to my heart though, when I am reminded; "Just as I am, Thou wilt receive, wilt welcome, pardon, cleanse, relieve."[6]

Jesus welcomes us into a close, intimate friendship with Him. We do not need to fear rejection. He promises that He will never cast us out.

> *All that the Father gives Me will come to Me, and who-ever comes to Me I will never cast out.* John 6:37.

Don't wait to come to the Lord for your daily devotions until you have everything together. He doesn't demand per-fection. We may feel the need to clean things up before feel-ing fit for His presence. Go to Him as you are: weak, help-less, unworthy, sinful – and let Him cleanse and purify you! No one else can atone for our sins; we certainly cannot our-selves. Don't be afraid to come to Him when you have failed. He who died for your sins knew all about your strug-gles before He called you to Himself.

> *For we do not have a high priest who is unable to sym-pathize with our weaknesses, but one who in every respect has been tempted as we are, yet without sin.* Hebrews 4:15.

Life is short. Now is the time to draw near to Him in close fellowship. Remember:

"If you tarry till you're better,
You will never come at all."

Let's be careful not to buy into the lie that we need to fix ourselves up first – just come to Him!

"Let not conscience make you linger,
Not of fitness fondly dream;
All the fitness He requireth
Is to feel your need of Him.[8]"

This doesn't in any way mean that we can become soft or accustomed towards sin. No! The more we are with Jesus, the more we develop a real hatred of sin and all that it entails. Our soul will begin to abhor anything that would mar our relationship with Him.

WITH A SPIRIT OF REPENTANCE

The prodigal son realized his sin and came back to his father in a spirit of repentance.

> *I will arise and go to my father, and I will say to him, "Father, I have sinned against heaven and before you. I am no longer worthy to be called your son. Treat me as one of your hired servants." And he arose and came to his father. But while he was still a long way off, his father saw him and felt compassion, and ran and embraced him and kissed him. And the son said to him, 'Father, I have sinned against heaven and before you. I am no longer worthy to be called your son.' But the father said to his servants, 'Bring quickly the best robe, and put it on him, and put a ring on his hand, and shoes on his feet. And bring the fattened calf and kill it, and let us eat and celebrate. For this my son was dead, and is alive again; he was lost, and is found.' And they began to celebrate.* Luke 15:18-24.

We also can rise and go to our Father when we have failed, confessing our sin, and trusting that He will receive us. He will cleanse away all of our sin by Christ's precious blood and will clothe us with His spotless robe of righteousness. He will not condemn us, but will receive us with open arms.

> *There is therefore now no condemnation for those who are in Christ Jesus.* Romans 8:1.

Don't Hold Back

Knowing this, why do we still hold back? What keeps us from coming to the Lord? Maybe we do not fully trust Him or count on His unchanging character, or thank Him for the abundant resources that He has offered to us. Instead, we just cower in the dark, burying our little seed of faith and hoarding the gifts that the Lord has given us, hoping to at least keep what little we feel we have for ourselves.

> *For it will be like a man going on a journey, who called his servants and entrusted to them his property. To one he gave five talents, to another two, to another one, to each according to his ability. Then he went away. He who had received the five talents went at once and traded with them, and he made five talents more. So also he who had the two talents made two talents more. But he who had received the one talent went and dug in the ground and hid his master's money. Now after a long time the master of those servants came and settled accounts with them. And he who had received the five talents came forward, bringing five talents more, saying, "Master, you delivered to me five talents; here I have made five talents more." His master said to him, "Well done, good and faithful servant. You have been faithful*

over a little; I will set you over much. Enter into the
joy of your master." And he also who had the two
talents came forward, saying, "Master, you delivered
to me two talents; here I have made two talents
more." His master said to him, "Well done, good
and faithful servant. You have been faithful over a lit-
tle; I will set you over much. Enter into the joy of
your master." He also who had received the one tal-
ent came forward, saying, "Master, I knew you to be
a hard man, reaping where you did not sow, and
gathering where you scattered no seed, so I was
afraid, and I went and hid your talent in the ground.
Here you have what is yours." But his master
answered him, "You wicked and slothful servant! You
knew that I reap where I have not sown and gather
where I scattered no seed? Then you ought to have
invested my money with the bankers, and at my com-
ing I should have received what was my own with
interest. So take the talent from him and give it to
him who has the ten talents. For to everyone who
has will more be given, and he will have an abun-
dance. But from the one who has not, even what he
has will be taken away. And cast the worthless ser-
vant into the outer darkness. In that place there will
be weeping and gnashing of teeth."
Matthew 25:14-30.

Somehow, we may allow ourselves to picture God as a stern judge looking down upon His children with displeasure.

Having this image in our minds will determine the way we live, as well as our relationship with the Lord. Like the man who was given only one talent, the way we think of the Lord will determine how He will respond to us.

With the merciful you show yourself merciful; with
the blameless man you show yourself blameless;
with the purified you show yourself pure; and with

the crooked you make yourself seem tortuous. For you save a humble people, but the haughty eyes you bring down. Psalm 18:25-27.

Once, I had a violin teacher who was extremely exacting and disciplined. Rarely would a smile cross her face. I grew to fear her displeasure and wondered if I could ever play a song perfectly in every detail as she required, though I did learn a lot of excellent techniques from her, and actually had fun trying to make her smile. Yet, somehow through that experience, I began to equate her strict requirements to what I thought God must be requiring of me. I felt that God must be like that: demanding perfection and showing His disapproval over any little mistake I made. So, as with my music practice, I thought, "I'll just have to try harder, determine to do my best to please God, and maybe someday I'll gain His approval."

What a depressing journey I was in for! If my violin techniques were perfect, but my music had no emotional depth, it sounded lifeless and dull. Similarly, I could never make my heart right out of my own effort. Even if my outward actions looked good, my heart was not right before God.

> *But we are all as an unclean thing, and all our righteousnesses are as filthy rags.*
> Isaiah 64:6. KJV

And then, when I could take it no longer, God's mercy lifted me up from the discouraging pit of my self-effort, into the rest and peace offered to those who fully trust in Him. As I poured out my troubles to my parents, I'll never forget what my dad told me. He reminded me that God is a loving father who does not look down on us just waiting for us to get out of line, so that He can knock us over the head. No! He is like a father who loves His children so much, no matter if they make a mistake or not. My mom explained how God loves me unconditionally – loving me without holding any conditions over my head. I didn't need to try to earn His love.

My mom so lovingly told me: "Dad and I love you just the way you are. Nothing you do could ever change that."

I was encouraged! As I pondered my parent's love and acceptance of their imperfect daughter, I realized how much more God must love me! My dad's compassion touched my heart and I was amazed how the Lord spoke to me through the following passage of Scripture:

> *The LORD is merciful and gracious, slow to anger and abounding in steadfast love. He will not always chide, nor will He keep His anger forever. He does not deal with us according to our sins, nor repay us according to our iniquities. For as high as the heavens are above the earth, so great is His steadfast love toward those who fear Him; as far as the east is from the west, so far does He remove our transgressions from us.* **As a father shows compassion to His children, so the LORD shows compassion to those who fear Him. For He knows our frame; He remembers that we are dust.**
> Psalm 103:8-14.

Knowing that God accepted me through Jesus alone, turned everything around. I no longer needed to strive to please Him by my own effort. I could rest in His provision, knowing that He provided a way for me to come to Him through the perfect sacrifice of His Son. There was nothing I could do to add to or subtract from His atonement. I was free to live for His pleasure!

LIVING FOR THE LORD'S PLEASURE

The blessed difference between all other religions and Christianity is that our acceptance before God doesn't depend on us – it depends on Christ alone. Nothing we can do or fail to do changes the way God looks at us. This doesn't give us the liberty to be inactive or disobedient. Instead, it motivates and inspires us to serve the One who takes delight in us. As those redeemed by Christ's blood, we have no reason to fear God's wrath any longer. Make sure that you are in Christ, for those who don't belong to Him have much to fear!

Take time to really get hold of the fact that God is pleased with YOU! He has created you just the way you are, and He has provided a way of salvation, so that you are fit to enjoy His presence. We now have freedom to live for the Lord's pleasure instead of suffering from the paralyzing effects of trying to please man.

> *The fear of man lays a snare, but whoever trusts in the LORD is safe.* Proverbs 29:25.

It gives the Lord pleasure when we revere Him and take Him at His Word, putting our sole hope and trust in His character – His steadfast, unshakeable, unmovable love. Our lives can be lived with the freeing knowledge and confidence that the Lord loves us, and we are accepted by Him. We can then live to please Jesus and not worry if other people are pleased with us or not.

> *His delight is not in the strength of the horse, nor His pleasure in the legs of a man, but the LORD takes pleasure in those who fear Him, in those who hope in His steadfast love.* Psalm 147:10-11.

When we are in Christ, the Lord looks on us with eternal pleasure. It is hard to comprehend or fathom all that it entails. God is not always pleased with what we do, but our position in His Son results in His great favor and delight. Jesus is God's beloved Son, in whom He is well pleased! God is eternal and unchanging, so His delight in those who are in Christ is eternal and unchanging.

> *By this I know that You delight in me: my enemy will not shout in triumph over me.* Psalm 41:11.

Here is how my dear fiancé, Zach, explains it: "Positionally we are in Christ; we are covered by His blood (our own sin atoned for, our negative balance is brought to 0, pretty good!), and robed in His own perfect righteousness (our 0 is brought up to 100%!). When God looks at us, He sees Christ's covering, and it is as if we never sinned at all. I am very conscious of my sin, and I come before the Lord weeping and repenting, brokenhearted for all of it, and (I say this reverently) God says, "What are you talking about? I don't know of any problem, I don't see anything as ever being on your record." Now, of course, He does know, but He has cast it all forever into the depths of the sea, "as far as the east is from the west"[9] (the two never meet), never to be remembered and brought against us. We are justified and reconciled."

Abide in <u>Jesus</u> – the perfect one. May this hope and joy settle in our hearts and lives, bringing forth glorious fruit resulting in praise to our Savior, a blessing to all those around us.

THE LORD DELIGHTS IN US

The LORD your God is with you, He is mighty to save. He will take great delight in you, He will quiet you with His love, He will rejoice over you with singing. Zephaniah 3:17. NIV

Can you picture the Lord rejoicing over you with singing? What song would He sing specifically for you, as He looks at you with eyes of great compassion and delight? Such loving pleasure should quiet our fearful, timid hearts with true hope and reassurance.

The Lord reassured His wayward people, who had been taken captive by other nations, of His great delight and pleasure in them, much like the expressed delight of a groom in his new bride.

You shall be a crown of beauty in the hand of the LORD, and a royal diadem in the hand of your God. You shall no more be termed Forsaken, and your land shall no more be termed Desolate, but you shall be called My Delight Is in Her, and your land Married; for the LORD delights in you, and your land shall be married. For as a young man marries a young woman, so shall your sons marry you, and as the bridegroom rejoices over the bride, so shall your God rejoice over you. Isaiah 62:3-5.

This beautiful truth should make us rejoice and reassure our timid, fearful hearts that the Lord does indeed delight in us and He accepts us in Christ, His beloved Son.

To the praise of the glory of His grace, wherein He hath made us accepted in the beloved.
Ephesians 1:6. KJV

CHAPTER 3

Approaching the Throne

BEFORE THE THRONE OF GOD ABOVE
By Charitie L. Bancroft

Before the throne of God above
I have a strong and perfect plea.
A great High Priest whose Name is Love
Who ever lives and pleads for me.
My name is graven on His hands,
My name is written on His heart.
I know that while in Heaven He stands
No tongue can bid me thence depart.

When Satan tempts me to despair
And tells me of the guilt within,
Upward I look and see Him there
Who made an end of all my sin.
Because the sinless Savior died
My sinful soul is counted free.
For God the just is satisfied
To look on Him and pardon me.

Behold Him there the risen Lamb,
My perfect spotless righteousness,
The great unchangeable I AM,
The King of glory and of grace,
One in Himself I cannot die.
My soul is purchased by His blood,
My life is hid with Christ on high,
With Christ my Savior and my God!

*Easter lilies: who would have thought that what had start-
ed out as an ugly, brown bulb would ever turn out to be so
gorgeous, fragrant, and pure white? In the dark nutrients of
the soil, there is all the potential for growing a plant.
Slowly, silently the green shoot starts to appear from the
brown, papery bulb. With careful watering – not too much
or too little, plenty of sunshine, and tender-loving care, a
bloom soon appears. It attracts much attention with its tan-
talizing fragrance and spotless purity. Lilies often mark the
celebration of Easter – the resurrection of our Lord Jesus
Christ. It is a symbol of His life and purity.*

As young ladies we want to become like Christ, clothed in
His spotless, purity. Like an Easter lily we want to be pure,
fresh, beautiful, and possessing the aroma of Christ. As
such, we will look different than the world, but wouldn't that
make us so happy and grateful to know that we stand out as
a bright, shining light for Christ?

The world encourages girls to be assertive, selfish, domi-
neering, brash, loud, aggressive, boastful, and to pursue
careers outside of the home. On the other hand, the Lord
desires His daughters to be willing to be humble, selfless,
submitting to authority, and cultivating a gentle, quiet spirit
that is beautiful in His sight. The Bible encourages women
to joyfully embrace the calling of being helpmeets to their
husbands, focusing on their families, and creating a beautiful
home atmosphere that is a haven of rest.

The modern clothing industry markets attire for even very
young girls that is immodest, sloppy, masculine, and even
seductive. Is this how a Christian woman should be arrayed
spiritually or physically?

> *Women should adorn themselves in respectable
> apparel, with modesty and self-control, not with
> braided hair and gold or pearls or costly attire, but
> with what is proper for women who profess godliness
> – with good works.* I Timothy 2:9-10.

A woman must not wear men's clothing, nor a man wear women's clothing, for the LORD your God detests anyone who does this. Deuteronomy 22:5.

It takes faith and trust to surrender this area of what we wear to the Lord. I'll admit that it is sometimes hard to find beautiful, modest clothing, but if we are willing to obey, the Lord will meet us halfway and abundantly supply our needs.

Take a look at the flowers that God has created in beautiful array. They do not fret, toil, or spin for their clothing, yet we cannot surpass them in their beauty! In a practical sense, the Lord graciously reminds us to give the area of clothing over to Him as our provider. He desires that we clothe ourselves with modest, feminine apparel that would display fresh purity – like a spotless Easter lily! When we are willing to obey His command for women to dress modestly, He will provide for us abundantly! It is fun and an adventure to be creative in finding or even making clothing that reflects our dear Savior and brings honor to His name. The way we dress does not secure a right relationship with the Lord or grant us His favor, but when we are walking in close fellowship with Him, we will see that it is so crucial that our outer lives bear testimony to His purity, grace, and Lordship in our lives.

Spiritually, we do not need to fret about our appearance before the Lord. What really matters to Him is our heart condition. When we approach the Holy One, we must come clothed in Christ's righteousness. If we take matters into our own hands, we will find that all of our righteous acts are as filthy rags compared to His spotless garments. Jesus has seen to it that we may have His pure righteousness for our attire. We can then confidently approach God's throne, not based on what we have done, but only through the blood of Jesus!

Therefore, brothers, since we have confidence to enter the holy places by the blood of Jesus, by the new and living way that He opened for us through the

curtain, that is, through His flesh, and since we have
a great priest over the house of God, let us draw near
with a true heart in full assurance of faith, with our
hearts sprinkled clean from an evil conscience and
our bodies washed with pure water. Let us hold fast
the confession of our hope without wavering, for He
who promised is faithful. Hebrews 10:19-23

JESUS OUR HIGH PRIEST

In the Jewish laws only the High Priest was allowed to enter the Most Holy Place and only once a year. (Heb. 9:7). It was a very serious thing to enter God's presence in the Most Holy Place. The High Priest had to make careful preparation to purify himself before he went behind the veil that separated the Holy Place from the Most Holy Place in the temple of God.

The High Priest could not enter without taking the blood of sacrificed bulls or goats.

A magnificent thing happened when Christ died on the cross. The curtain or veil of the temple was torn in two from top to bottom. (Mark 15:38.) Only the all-powerful hand of God could have done such a thing! At the moment of Christ's death the complete sacrifice was made so that our evil hearts may be cleansed by His shed blood, and we may then enter into His holy presence.

Christ offered the perfect atonement for our sins once and for all. His sacrifice ushers us into God's holy presence cleansed and clothed in His righteousness. We no longer need to fear God's just wrath or condemnation. We are accepted through Jesus, God's beloved Son.

So, let us come to Him with gratitude, humility, and confidence. Confidence literally means "with faith." We can approach God's throne with faith that he will accept us in Jesus. It is not a wishful uncertainty; it is a sure reality!

Draw near to God with a true, sincere heart in full assurance of faith. Why do we often hold back from entering into

God's presence? Sometimes we are afraid that He is not
pleased with what He will see. We may feel dirty and
unworthy to approach Christ in His pure light.

As I mentioned before, don't try and clean yourself up
first. He is the only one who can wash away your sins.
Come to Him so that He can make you clean.

> "What can wash away my sins? NOTHING
> (absolutely nothing!) but the blood of Jesus."[10]

As we come into His light, He will reveal sins that need to
be confessed. What we need to do is come, since Jesus
knows all about our sins anyway. We can come to Jesus just
as we are and receive His true cleansing. His blood can
wash our guilty consciences as white as snow.

We can come confidently before His throne, because we
have a Great High Priest, Jesus Christ, who has provided the
way by the shedding of His own blood. We are always wel-
comed through Jesus.

> *Consequently, He is able to save to the uttermost*
> *those who draw near to God through Him, since He*
> *always lives to make intercession for them.*
> Hebrews 7:25.

Jesus, who is our High Priest, has made it possible for us
to come before the Lord as priests ourselves.

> *You yourselves like living stones are being built up as*
> *a spiritual house, to be a holy priesthood, to offer*
> *spiritual sacrifices acceptable to God through Jesus*
> *Christ.* I Peter 2:5.

We who are made priests in turn are called to proclaim the
greatness of God by giving testimony that we have been
delivered from darkness and have been brought into the glorious light of His presence.

Dear sisters, since all has been done to make the way clear for us to approach God's throne, let's not hold back. Come to Him confidently – with faith, knowing that the price is paid, our hearts are cleansed, and the Lord is pleased.

The fullness of joy that He offers when we come into His presence is incomparable to anything else we could enjoy here on earth. The Lord will offer us His blessed peace.

RECEIVING CHRIST'S BLESSED PEACE

I remember vividly one crisp, October day a year ago. I was feeling quite emotional. Things weren't turning out as I had hoped, and I felt all out of sorts. My family and I were eagerly waiting to hear news from my sister and brother-in-law (who are serving the Lord in Asia) about the arrival of their first child. Mom and I both longed to be with Melissa instead of wondering how she was handling her first time of being in labor. We fervently prayed that nothing would go wrong.

That same week I was house sitting for some friends, the Montes, who lived nearby. Originally I had pictured that my time staying at their house and caring for their animals would be like a mini-retreat, getting away from things for awhile to be able to think, pray, and write. Instead, I was quite busy and felt like I wasn't accomplishing much. I certainly wasn't getting the quiet time that I had hoped for. I was worn out and completely out of sorts, though I felt terrible about my attitude. So I did what most girls do: I went up to my room and had a good cry, praying and asking for the Lord's grace, help, and forgiveness.

My mom soon found me though, and I was greatly encouraged as she helped me look at things with a better perspective. She empathized with how I felt, saying that she has gone through days that are frustrating, making you want to just go to bed and start all over again. It helped to look at things more practically. Thank the Lord for mothers who give wise counsel to their daughters!

When I got back to the Monte's lovely house to stay that night, I took my Bible and sat down at their big dining room table. I decided to turn some music on. The CD that was already in their player intrigued me. It was entitled "Blessed Peace" by the Fuller Family. That surely was what I needed: a good serving of some blessed peace.

As the music began to play, and Anne Fuller's rich voice began to sing, I sat spellbound. The words of the song described my feelings and thoughts exactly.

Here are the lovely words, though I wish you could hear them being sung by Anne Fuller's beautiful voice:

BLESSED PEACE
By Anne Fuller

Now sit still and all are sleeping
And I find a place for quiet prayer.
For I find my heart is heavy
And the cares have made me weary,
And I need my Father near.

I bow my head and tell Him
All the sorrows of my day.
I tell Him how I failed again,
Confessing all my sins
And as the tears run down my face,
What marvelous grace,
I can feel my Father near.

Refrain:
And my heart becomes the very throne room,
Where I kneel at my Savior's feet,
And I feel His love surround me,
As He gives His blessed peace.

As I kneel there in the quiet
All my sorrows they grow small,
And my weary heart is strengthened
And my sins He's forgiven them all
And as I lift His name in praise,
What marvelous grace
I can feel my Father near.[11]

This song, among many others in this book, has ministered to me greatly as I have sought to spend time seeking the Lord's face. Melodious music and heartfelt words can lift the spirit and touch the heart like nothing else. When King Saul was greatly troubled, the only thing that could soothe his tormented mind was David's peaceful harp music. In the dark night of our soul the Lord often gives us songs in the night.

On that October day I keenly sensed the Lord's presence as He spoke to me through the words of the song that Anne Fuller had penned. Yet, it isn't always that we will be able to "feel" the Lord's presence. The horrific result of Adam and Eve's sin was spiritual death – separation from the presence of their loving Creator. How it must have grieved the Father's heart to have His children banished from His holy presence! To think that now His Son is preparing a place for those who are relying on His atoning blood for their salvation - a place that we may be with Him and the Father forever!

We will not be able to realize and enjoy the full blessings of being in the Lord's glorious presence until we shed this earthly tent of our body and are given glorious heavenly bodies to dwell forever with Him. Now we have the need for faith. We must come to Him believing that He is and that He rewards those who seek Him.

> *And without faith it is impossible to please Him, for whoever would draw near to God must believe that He exists and that He rewards those who seek Him.*
> Hebrews 11:6.

THE UPWARD CALL OF GOD

Even just the small glimpses of the Lord's glory that are revealed to us in Christ and His Word are life transforming. So, let us seek to know Him more, but remember that knowing the Lord will cost us something. Read the following passage slowly and make it your prayer too:

> *Indeed, I count everything as loss because of the surpassing worth of knowing Christ Jesus my Lord. For His sake I have suffered the loss of all things and count them as rubbish, in order that I may gain Christ, and be found in Him, not having a righteousness of my own that comes from the law, but that which comes through faith in Christ, the righteousness from God that depends on faith – that I may know Him and the power of His resurrection, and may share His sufferings, becoming like Him in His death, that by any means possible I may attain the resurrection from the dead. Not that I have already obtained this or am already made perfect, but I press on to make it my own, because Christ Jesus has made me His own. Brothers, I do not consider that I have made it my own. But one thing I do: forgetting what lies behind and straining forward to what lies ahead, I press on toward the goal for the prize of the upward call of God in Christ.* Philippians 3:8-14.

What ONE thing must we do to obtain the richest prize of knowing Christ? Forgetting what is behind and straining forward to what lies ahead, which really is just one action. Repentance is a 180° turn: turning from the past, so that we can move towards what is ahead. Wherever you are in your walk with Jesus, you can leave your faults, failures, mistakes, and sins behind you so that you may move forward – upward – heavenward! The Christian life is the most freeing, positive, and optimistic life there is! We do not need psychologists to help us deal with our past; we do not need self-esteem to boost our self image – we just need Jesus! We need Him to be our focus, our goal, our life! Not just in a manner of speaking, but in reality. We easily sit around and talk about how we long to know Him, but do we really? Do we count ALL rubbish in comparison to knowing Him? Are we experiencing the real freedom that comes from living our lives focused on the single pursuit of knowing Christ?

It may not be that the Lord will ask you to sell all of your possessions or do something "magnificent" for others to see. It may be that the Spirit is gently calling you to SPEND (yes, it will cost you something) some time seeking the Lord in secret - just you and your Bible where no one else can see. As you approach the Lord's throne, kneel in humility before His righteous presence. Bring Him your praise; bring Him your burdens; bring Him your joy; bring Him your sorrow. You will receive a great reward, for there is absolutely nothing compared to the joy of being in God's presence, receiving His love and guidance directly from His precious Word.

As we come to this great and loving God, we will find that He is looking for one response from our hearts – worshipful love. No one else is worthy of our highest love and devotion. He alone is worthy of our worship, adoration, reverence, and respect.

> *But the hour is coming, and is now here, when the true worshipers will worship the Father in spirit and truth, for the Father is seeking such people to worship Him. God is spirit, and those who worship Him must worship in spirit and truth.* John 4:23-24.

CHAPTER 4

A Heart of Worship

THY MIGHT SETS FAST THE MOUNTAINS
The Psalter 1912

Thy might sets fast the mountains; strength girds Thee evermore
To calm the raging peoples and still the ocean's roar.
Thy majesty and greatness are through all lands confessed,
And joy on earth Thou sendest afar, from east to west.

To bless the earth Thou sendest from Thy abundant store
The waters of the springtime, enriching it once more.
The seed by Thee provided is sown over hill and plain,
And Thou with gentle showers dost bless the springing grain.

The year with good Thou crownest, the earth Thy mercy fills,
The wilderness is fruitful, and joyful are the hills;
With corn the vales are covered, the flocks in pastures graze;
All nature joins in singing a joyful song of praise.

All night the clouds have hovered close, enveloping Queen Mountain in a dewy comforter. The mist graces each feathery tamarack branch with a string of pearly dewdrops. The stillness of the gloaming is broken for awhile as the mournful, lonely sound of the approaching train whistle echoes through the mountains in the moist night air. The train rumbles over the tracks and across the trestle of the Twin Bridges. The damp smell of old pine needles gives a spicy odor to the fresh mountain air.

Soon the sun begins to rise. The vapor gradually disappears from sight. The bright rays of sunshine make the clouds retreat to reveal a clear blue sky which sets off the greenish, purple mountains. The damp earth begins to dry off in the warm sunshine. One can almost feel the warmth arise from the forest floor. The dew sparkles like diamonds on the bright red kinnickinnic berries and the tall sweetgrass. The huckleberry bushes are heavy-laden with purple, juicy berries.

"The sun streaming through the mountains" seems to reflect its golden rays on the quivering aspen leaves. The lodgepole pines stand erect like steeples, pointing heavenward, as a mountain bluebird perches in the high branches. Its song can be barely heard over the constant, musical roar of the Moyie River as it tumbles over the rocks on its way to the Kootenai.

The crystal clear water rushes and plummets as the river winds its way down, heading towards the small town of Bonners Ferry that is cozily nestled among the mountains.

The breathtaking awe of beholding the majestic mountains produces a song of praise to our Heavenly Father from a heart of sincere worship and adoration, as we marvel at what His mighty hand has made.

I have found the book of Exodus to be a beautiful lesson in following the Lord, as it shows us how the Lord desires His people to worship Him.

You have led in Your steadfast love the people whom You have redeemed; You have guided them by Your strength to Your holy abode. You will bring them in and plant them on Your holy mountain, the place, O Lord, which Your hands have established. The Lord will reign forever and ever. Exodus 15:13, 17-18.

The Israelites came before the mountain and Moses went to meet with the Lord who instructed him to tell the Israelites:

"You yourselves have seen what I did to the Egyptians, and how I bore you on eagle's wings and brought you to Myself..." Exodus 19:4.

Look at the great lengths the Lord took to bring His people to ***Himself***! He performed mighty deeds and brought the Israelites out of their bondage, triumphantly! He lifted them above every impossible, difficult situation and bore them on eagle's wings ~ to ***Himself***!

I am amazed to see this picture coming out so clearly of God's passion for His glory and His purpose for the people, whom He created, to be worshipping Him and enjoying His presence.

"Now therefore, if you will indeed obey My voice and keep My covenant, you shall be My treasured possession among all peoples, for all the earth is Mine; and you shall be to Me a kingdom of priests and a holy nation." Exodus 19:5-6.

Christians have this wonderful privilege too, of being God's royal priesthood and a holy (set apart) nation. We are His ***treasured possession***!

But you are a chosen race, a royal priesthood, a holy nation, a people for His own possession (Why? So that we might selfishly enjoy this position and the benefits – excluding ourselves from others? No!) *that you may proclaim the excellencies of Him who called you out of darkness into His marvelous light...* I Peter 2:9

God calls us to be His own to cause even the Gentiles (unbelievers) to glorify Him. We are to proclaim His incredible attributes, the excellent way He redeemed us, and what He has saved us from.

> *Beloved, I urge you as sojourners and exiles to abstain from the passions of the flesh, which wage war against your soul. Keep your conduct among the Gentiles honorable, so that when they speak against you as evildoers, they may see your good deeds and glorify God on the day of visitation.* I Peter 2:11-12.

Moses was instructed to consecrate the people for the Lord's appearing. Yet they could not even touch the mountain or enter the Lord's presence.

> *For you have not come to what may be touched... But you have come to Mount Zion and to God, the judge of all...and to Jesus, the mediator of a new covenant... See that you do not refuse Him who is speaking... Therefore let us be grateful for receiving a kingdom that cannot be shaken, and thus let us offer to God acceptable worship, with reverence and awe, for our God is a consuming fire.* Select verses from Hebrews 12:18-29.

Oh, may He consume all that is not pleasing to Him in my life! This brings fear and trembling to think of God's holiness and wrath. Yet, no longer am I an object of His wrath because of the blood of Jesus.

> *...we all once lived in the passions of our flesh, carrying out the desires of the body and the mind, and were by nature children of wrath, like the rest of*

mankind. But God, being rich in mercy, because of the great love with which He loved us, even when we were dead in our trespasses, made us alive together with Christ— by grace you have been saved— and raised us up with Him and seated us with Him in the heavenly places in Christ Jesus, so that in the coming ages He might show the immeasurable riches of His grace in kindness toward us in Christ Jesus.
Ephesians 2:3-7.

We do not need to fear the Lord's wrath which has been appeased by Jesus's sufficient sacrifice. Yet, there is a fear that we do need to have – a reverential fear. Not a fear that cringes with the expectation of discipline, but a fear that honors, respects, and holds in high regard the object of one's affections. This type of fear motivates us to turn from our sin.

Moses said to the people, "Do not fear, for God has come to test you, that the fear of Him may be before you, that you may not sin." Exodus 20:20.

WORSHIP FROM THE HEART

What was the destination of the Israelites, God's chosen people? Was it not to the Promised Land that the Lord brought His people out of their bondage and slavery in Egypt – a land that had all of the physical benefits and blessings that every human longs for? Peace from one's enemies, a secure dwelling, health, and happiness. Wasn't this the ultimate goal that God's people were encouraged to attain?

No, all of these side benefits were just the result of God's higher purpose for them. Yes, He moved His mighty hand of wonders to save them from a land of bondage and tyranny, but His purpose was so that they would be free to worship Him. Their destination was His holy abode – the sanctuary of His presence. God Himself was the answer to Israel's burdened, longing heart. He had heard their cry for freedom and it touched His heart, yet God sees beyond the temporal and looks beneath the surface to the real need. He gives the real answer

– Himself. As humans, bound by physical time and temporary things, it is so easy to not go beyond to recognize the spiritual need or to contemplate the eternal. Thus we have the admonition to walk by faith and not by what we see.

> *So we are always of good courage. We know that while we are at home in the body we are away from the Lord, for we walk by faith, not by sight.*
> II Corinthians 5:6-7.

Faith goes beyond our feelings. It is more than sensing that "someone is there." It is a solid belief and trust that God exists and that he will do what He has promised.

In our quiet times of worship we should keep this in mind: that the Lord has delivered us to worship Him. We are delivered from fear, sin, depression, darkness, discouragement, and from whatever terrible state we were in before we gave our hearts and lives to be governed by the Lord's supreme reign. Now we have the freedom to enjoy God's presence and all of His wonderful benefits – His glorious light, as well as encouragement, confidence, joy, and righteousness. We are free to worship the Lord.

THE CENTRALITY OF WORSHIP

What exactly is worship? Worship is declaring God's worthiness by our reverence and adoration of Him. It is enjoying Him for who He is.

The Puritans had a profound understanding of this. "The Valley of Vision: A Collection of Puritan Prayers and Devotions," is an excellent book that inspires worshipful prayers.

> "I have known men who come to God for nothing else but just to come to Him, they so loved Him. They scorned to soil Him and themselves with any other errand than just purely to be alone with Him in His presence."
> ~Thomas Goodwin, the Puritan.[12]

Taking your hymnal out during your quiet time is also

very helpful. There are many wonderful, Scriptural truths portrayed in the old hymns, that are like treasures to be rediscovered with each generation.

We have to be careful that we don't always equate worship with music. We can worship the Lord with reverent music and singing, but worship goes far beyond that. Go directly to God's Word for inspiration to worship Him.

> "Endless material for worship is enshrined in divine revelation, for worship is simply the adoring contemplation of God as He has been pleased to reveal Himself in His Son and in the Scriptures, especially in the Psalms, the inspired book of prayer."[13]

I have enjoyed reading through the book of Psalms in one month. A neat pattern to follow is to read one out of every thirty Psalms in correlation with the date. So, for example, if today is the 10th of the month, then I would read Psalm 10, 40, 70, 100, and 130. It is amazing that the Psalms seem to fit so well together when they are read that way.

Spending time alone with the Lord outside in His creation is very helpful for focusing on our Wise Creator. We can learn more about His character as we observe the things He has made, though we learn much more from reading His Word. We want to cultivate a worshipful attitude that cherishes God's Word.

> "God granted a glorious, although only partial, revelation of Himself in the wonders of His creation. 'The heavens are telling of the glory of God,' wrote David. 'And their expanse is declaring the work of His hands' (Psalm 19:1) From His inconceivably vast universe, we can learn something of His majesty, infinite power and wisdom, beauty and orderliness.
> The heavens declare Thy glory, Lord,
> In every star Thy wisdom shines;
> But when our eyes behold Thy Word,
> We read Thy name in fairer lines.
> Isaac Watts

But the heavens do not declare the mercy and love of God. Only in the face of Jesus Christ do we see the full blaze of the divine glory, for 'it was the Father's good pleasure for all the fullness to dwell in Him' (Col. 1:19). No worship that ignores Christ is acceptable to God, for it is only through Him that we can know and have access to the Father."[14]

Worship is a lifestyle of love, service, and abiding in Christ. It isn't just a thought, or a duty performed at a certain time or in a certain place. The Lord wants us to love with all that we are: heart, soul, and strength.

"We should, however, beware of conceiving of worship as being confined solely to the realm of thought, for in Scripture it is linked with service. "You shall worship the LORD your God and serve Him only,' were our Lord's words to Satan (Matt. 4:10). We should not separate what God has joined. Worship is no substitute for service, nor is service a substitute for worship. But true worship must always be expressed in loving service."[15]

It is a sacred, holy thing to worship our Infinite, Holy God. Worship is to be sincere, not for show; humble, not arrogant; fresh, not stale; spiritual, not fleshly; true, not false. Let us seek to worship the Lord in the splendor of His holiness, finding that He alone is worthy.

Worshipping the Lord is a corporate act, as well as a solitary thing. It is a beautiful thing when we learn how to worship the Lord in our everyday lives outside of church. Jesus is present with us everywhere, so let's purpose to sing in the shadow of His loving presence.

CHAPTER 5

Singing in the Shadow of His Presence

THE SECRET OF HIS PRESENCE
By Ellen L. Goreh

In the secret of His presence
How my soul delights to hide:
Oh, how precious are the lessons
Which I learn at Jesus' side.
Earthly cares can only vex me,
Trials never lay me low,
And when Satan comes to tempt me,
To the secret place I go.

When my soul is faint and thirsty,
'Neath the shadow of His wing
There is a cool and pleasant shelter,
And a fresh and crystal spring.
And my Savior rests beside me,
As we hold communion sweet;
If I tried, I could not utter
What He says, when thus we meet.

Only this: I know, I tell Him
All my doubts, and griefs, and fears;
Oh, how patiently He listens,
And my drooping heart He cheers.
Do you think He ne'er reproves me?
What a false friend He would be,
If He never, never told me
Of the faults which He must see.

Do you think that I could love Him
Half so well, or as I ought,
If He did not plainly tell me
Each displeasing word and thought?
No! for He is very faithful,
And that makes me trust Him more,
For I know that He doth love me,
Though sometimes He wounds me sore.

Would you like to know the sweetness
Of this secret of the Lord?
Go and hide beneath His shadow,
This shall then be your reward.
And whene'er you leave the silence
Of this happy meeting place,
You must mind and bear the image
Of the Master in your face.

Silently the moon shines its reflected light on a sleeping world below. All of the starry host glistens like diamonds on the velvety backdrop of the cloudless, night sky. God so beautifully designed the night-time darkness for rest and sleep.

Nothing is quite as irksome though, as a sleepless night. The minutes tick by so slowly as you toss and turn. Somehow your mind doesn't agree with your tired body as it actively processes the day's events or plans out tomorrow's course – often with much worry and care.

Darkness and night typifies loneliness, sorrow, weariness, shadows, trials, uncertainty, agonizing endurance, or a clouded vision. It is common for children to be afraid of the dark or what it may be concealing. Darkness is often a picture of evil, secrecy, lurking danger, fear…

God created the night for peace, rest, and refreshment. Man has used the night to cover up evil, or to be spent in miserable fretting.

If you lie down, you will not be afraid; when you lie down, your sleep will be sweet. Do not be afraid of sudden terror or of the ruin of the wicked, when it comes, for the LORD will be your confidence and will keep your foot from being caught. Proverbs 3:24-26.

The Lord created darkness to help facilitate sleep. Yet, we are not left without any light, for the Lord saw fit to create lesser lights to rule the night. The velvety darkness reminds us to rest and offers a backdrop for the beautiful starlit sky. In a spiritual sense we all were in darkness before the Lord shed His glorious light into our lives by sending us Jesus as our Savior.

The people who walked in darkness have seen a great light; those who dwelt in a land of deep darkness, on them has light shined. For to us a Child is born, to us a Son is given; and the government shall be upon His shoulder, and His name shall be called Wonderful Counselor, Mighty God, Everlasting Father, Prince of Peace. Of the increase of His government and of peace there will be no end. Isaiah 9:2, 6-7.

IN HIS PRESENCE

How easily people take for granted God's presence and dominion over the earth. The most terrible thing about hell is being separated from God's loving, sustaining presence. For in Him alone do we truly *"live and move and have our being."* Acts 17:28.

All of our needs are met in Him. When He reigns in our life, taking wise control, there is real peace, because He is the Prince of Peace. Jesus endured being separated from His Father's presence for our sake, so that we may enter in God's presence clothed with Christ's righteousness. One of the greatest blessings we receive from the Lord is His promised presence.

One summer day, when I was about 5 or 6 years old, I

learned, even though it was just for a short while, what it feels like to be alone and insecure. It was a sunny day at Deer Trail Lodge, the resort my parents owned in the north woods of Wisconsin. I felt quite grown up and independent, though, I wasn't very old.

I loved playing in our woods, or up in the meadow above our driveway/parking area. There was always something new to discover about God's creation as I observed nature. The woods, lake, and the whole outdoors were our play-ground. My sister, brother, and I practically lived outdoors all summer. One could tell by my sun-bleached hair and tan face and arms. It was a wonderful place for an inquisitive little girl to grow and learn, though it was a lot of work for my parents.

Each day Mom would hike down our half-mile long driveway with my older sister, younger brother, and me. Our driveway always seemed much longer to our short, childlike legs. We loved to dawdle on the way, tracing each other's footprints in the sand with a stick, or collecting rocks, or observing the miniature canyons and crevices that the previous night's rain had etched in our driveway by the rushing water.

Though the big trees in the dark woods towered over our house and lodge, I always felt secure, knowing that my dad or mom were always there.

This particular day was busy, as usual, which didn't concern my little mind, but mom didn't have time to take a hike down the driveway to get the mail that day, so she decided to take us with her in our navy station wagon. I was too occupied in my play to want to interrupt myself by going down to the mailbox. Mom agreed that I could stay behind, since she would be gone just a few minutes, and I assured her that I would be fine. I felt pretty independent and had no worries as Mom, Melissa, and Danny drove out of sight.
Yet, when they had disappeared, it suddenly felt like a cloud had covered the sunshine and I felt so alone – the realization that they were gone quickly sunk in. The woods seemed

very dark, the driveway looked so long and winding in my mother's absence. I was ALL ALONE! I had always enjoyed getting away by myself outside, but that was because of the unconscious awareness that my mom was close at hand. Her presence was always near and felt, even when I couldn't see her. But now I was left behind and the lonely minutes seemed to stretch on forever as I strained to see the returning vehicle come in sight.

"Mom!" I cried out in a helpless voice, choked with tears, knowing that she couldn't even hear me. Quietly I began to pray through my tears. My independence, security, and carefree play seemed to have vanished when my mom had disappeared from sight.

Until, there they were – what a wonderful sight!!! Though it seemed long, it really was only a few minutes before they came back. Mom was quite astonished to see her young daughter's tear-stained face when they came back, which had just moments ago been smiling and happy.

"Why, Teresa, what is wrong? We weren't gone long! You knew that we'd be right back!" My mom's voice was filled with compassionate surprise. I'm not sure now what I said as I swallowed my tears, but I do know that I was SO happy to see Mom! She was back and everything was all right. My fear seemed quite irrational, though it was very real. After this, I decided to stick with my mom and not be so self-reliant. It was no fun being left alone, anyway!

The Dictionary's definition of "presence" is: "The existence of a person or thing in a certain place; opposed to absence." "A being in company near or before the face of another." "Approach face to face or nearness of a great personage." "State of being in view; sight."[16]

Unlike enjoying the presence of other people, we must keep in mind that God's presence isn't limited to any one place at any one time. We can't literally see Christ at this time, but those who are redeemed, considered righteous in

His sight, can behold Him through eyes of faith as we learn about His character from God's Word.

> *For the LORD is righteous; He loves righteous deeds; the upright shall behold His face.* Psalm 7:11.

God's presence is so far-reaching. We can never escape from His presence here on earth. We can rest assured that the Lord will be with us and will safely lead us to our heavenly home, the place where his presence is fully known.

> *Whither shall I go from Thy spirit? Or whither shall I flee from Thy presence? If I ascend up into heaven, Thou art there: if I make my bed in hell, behold, Thou art there. If I take the wings of the morning, and dwell in the uttermost parts of the sea; even there shall Thy hand lead me, and Thy right hand shall hold me. If I say, Surely the darkness shall cover me; even the night shall be light about me. Yea, the darkness hideth not from Thee; but the night shineth as the day: the darkness and the light are both alike to Thee.* Psalm 139:7-12. KJV

We can experience a taste of heaven here on earth. True heaven on earth is when God's presence and character is known and felt through our spiritual senses. There is nothing as joyous or utterly fulfilling as experiencing moments in God's presence. It is beyond description or any earthly experience.

THE JOY OF HIS PRESENCE

The most fragrant fruit that will be produced as a result of our devotion in spending time with Jesus, will be joy – a sweet, full, sunny, contagious joy - a joy that the world cannot have nor will ever understand.

*You make known to me the path of life; in Your **presence** there is fullness of joy; at Your right hand are pleasures forevermore.* Psalm 16:11.

Full, lasting joy is found only in one place – the presence of God. We can enjoy it in part while we are here on earth, but in heaven we will know the full extent of this incredible, indescribable joy.

CONVICTION IN HIS PRESENCE

*You have set our iniquities before You, our secret sins in the light of Your **presence**.* Psalm 90:8.

When we are in the Lord's presence we mustn't resist His conviction, but should allow the light of His Holy Spirit to illumine our lives and show us our sins. We then must confess and acknowledge our sins to Him, so we may enjoy closer, sweeter, and purer fellowship with our holy and gracious Lord. He will be faithful to forgive and cleanse us of our sins.

> *This then is the message which we have heard of Him, and declare unto you, that God is light, and in Him is no darkness at all. If we say that we have fellowship with Him, and walk in darkness, we lie, and do not tell the truth: But if we walk in the light, as He is in the light, we have fellowship one with another, and the blood of Jesus Christ His Son cleanseth us from all sin. If we say that we have no sin, we deceive ourselves, and the truth is not in us. If we confess our sins, He is faithful and just to forgive us our sins, and to cleanse us from all unrighteousness. If we say that we have not sinned, we make Him a liar, and His word is not in us.*
> I John 1:5-10. KJV

When we confess our sins to Jesus, we can trust that God will not condemn us or cast us from His presence.

WITH THANKSGIVING

> *Let us come into His **presence** with thanksgiving; let us make a joyful noise to Him with songs of praise!* Psalm 95:2.

This is how we should approach the Lord's presence; with thanksgiving and songs of praise! We should begin each day by declaring the Lord's steadfast love in the morning. This will help us "keep on the sunny side of life." At the close of the day, it is a beautiful thing to reflect on God's faithfulness that He shows throughout the day.

> *It is good to give thanks to the LORD, to sing praises to Your name, O Most High; to declare Your steadfast love in the morning, and Your faithfulness by night.* Psalm 92:1-2.

His faithfulness is great. It is good to meditate on it as we come to rest after a full day of busyness and earthly cares. Often it is the little, every day blessings of God that we take for granted. He so faithfully causes the sun and rain to nourish our land each day. He so faithfully supplies us food to eat, and quenches our thirst each day. He gives us the air to breathe, our eyes to see, and our hearts to enjoy…

Let us not grow so accustomed to the little everyday gifts that we forget to thank the Lord for them. Sing His praises and declare His faithfulness at the close of every day, saying, "Lord, You are good and have proved Yourself so faithful once again." May we not grow callous to the rich blessings that He bestows on us everyday!

MEDITATE ON GOD AND HIS WORD

The first Psalm gives us an example of a godly person. One of the key qualities that are displayed is the love of Scripture and the earnest desire of meditating on it day and night.

*But his delight is in the law of the LORD; and in
His law doth he meditate day and night.* Psalm 1:2.

Instead of mindlessly "counting sheep," we can turn our
hearts to the treasure store of God's Word and meditate on
His instruction. It is so wise to memorize Scripture for
such times when we most need it.

*My soul will be satisfied as with fat and rich food,
and my mouth will praise You with joyful lips, when
I remember You upon my bed, and meditate on you
in the watches of the night; for You have been my
help, and in the shadow of Your wings I will sing
for joy. My soul clings to You; Your right hand
upholds me.* Psalm 63:5-8.

In the worries of a sleepless night remember the Lord and
meditate on Him. Consider His character, the wonders He
has performed in your life, His provision for you in Jesus...
soon you will discover that a song of praise will begin to
form in your heart. He is our ever-present help and causes
us to sing for joy under His sustaining presence. It gives our
hearts deeper trust and sweeter joy to take time to meditate
on the Lord.

*My meditation of Him shall be sweet: I will be glad
in the LORD.* Psalm 104:34. KJV

A LINGERING MELODY

One day as I was putting my violin away after playing for
the residents at a local nursing home, an encouraging lady
told me, "your music will linger with us even after you go."
Her words touched me, and it was sweet to know that a song
was left in her heart.

*By day the LORD commands His steadfast love, and
at night His song is with me, a prayer to the God of
my life.* Psalm 42:8.

God provides for our needs and meets them fully in the person of Jesus Christ. The Lord is our song. His presence is with us – even when we are lonely, or anxious and cannot sleep.

Behold, God is my salvation; I will trust, and not be afraid: for the LORD JEHOVAH is my strength and my song; He also is become my salvation.
Isaiah 12:2.KSV

Some of the most lovely songs and hymns have been written out of the dark travail of the soul, the anguish that produces the sweetest strain of heavenly music. The Lord gives these melodies to bring us comfort in sorrow.

But none says, "Where is God my Maker, who gives songs in the night." Job 35:10.

The Lord's song lingers with us into the night, often composed in the form of a prayer. The middle of the night is usually not the time that we do much singing, yet as we abide in His shadow, we can have songs in the night.

He that dwelleth in the secret place of the Most High shall abide under the shadow of the Almighty. He shall cover thee with His feathers, and under His wings shalt thou trust: His truth shall be thy shield and buckler. Thou shalt not be afraid for the terror by night; nor for the arrow that flieth by day; nor for the pestilence that walketh in darkness; nor for the destruction that wasteth at noonday.
Psalm 91:1, 4-6. KJV

So often our problems can look bigger at night than during the day. Just like shadows, which can exaggerate the true size of an object, the night can magnify the size of our troubles. At these times, my mom has often wisely reminded me that, "things will look different in the morning," and more often than not, they do! Fear magnifies, but perfect love casts out fear.

As a child, trusting securely in my parents' love and protection, excluded any cause for fear. When we lived in the deep, dark north woods of Wisconsin, I remember arriving home at night sometimes and noticing how very dark it was as we approached our home. One could almost feel the darkness. Mom and us children would wait trustingly in our station wagon as my dad would go out into the darkness to turn on some lights in the house. It was a very secure feeling to be safe in our car and to trust my father's protective care for us, as well as my mom's comforting presence. Inevitably one of us kids would still be sleeping, and Dad would have to carry us inside.

When we are dwelling surrendered in the shelter of God's sovereign control over our lives, we do not need to fear the terrors of the night, things that disturb, annoy, worry, or torment us, like a deadly disease (pestilence) that stalks in the darkness.

TRUSTING GOD'S CONTROL

The day is Thine, the night also is Thine: Thou hast prepared the light and the sun. Psalm 74:16. KJV

During the night-time of our soul, we may feel that our lives are out of control and that the Lord has somehow distanced Himself from our situation. Like Asaph we may cry out:

> *O God, why do You cast us off forever? Why does Your anger smoke against the sheep of your pasture? Remember Your congregation, which You have purchased of old, which You have redeemed to be the tribe of Your heritage! Remember Mount Zion, where You have dwelt.* Psalm 74:1-2.

Somehow we may feel that the Lord has forgotten us. Yet, God in no way forgets His children. How could He forget those whom His own Son came to save? He will never forget those who have been purchased by the precious, cost-ly blood of His beloved Son, Jesus Christ.

> *But Zion said, "The LORD has forsaken me; my Lord has forgotten me." Can a woman forget her nursing child, that she should have no compassion on the son of her womb? Even these may forget, yet I will not forget you. Behold, I have engraved you on the palms of My hands; your walls are continually before Me.*
> Isaiah 49:14-16.

God, as the initiator of the new covenant in Christ, has committed our well-being to His care. He has permanently engraved us on the palms of His hands. His seal of owner-ship is on His children, and it cannot be revoked.

Our circumstances may seem to dictate otherwise. Our lives may seem to be out of control. Yet we may rest assured knowing that the One who established the stars and sun, and who controls the day and night is very capable managing our situation. Let us trust God's wisdom and care. We need to take our erring hands off of our circumstances and let Him take over, saying, "Lord, this problem is Yours." The responsibility is really His, not ours, so trust Him!

Be willing to walk by faith in the darkness. When our sense of direction fails, or our feelings begin to lead us astray, let us turn to the ever-present, unchanging Word of God and find comfort and clear direction for our way. God's Word is a light for our path, guiding us step-by-step.

GOD KNOWETH
By Mrs. Mary G. Brainard
Changed by Philip P. Bliss

I know not what awaits me,
God kindly veils mine eyes,
And o'er each step of my onward way
He makes new scenes to rise;
And every joy He sends me, comes
A sweet and glad surprise.

Where He may lead I'll follow,
My trust in Him repose;
And every hour in perfect peace
I'll sing, He knows, He knows.

One step I see before me,
'Tis all I need to see,
The light of heaven more brightly shines,
When earth's illusions flee;
And sweetly through the silence, came
His loving, "Follow Me."

O blissful lack of wisdom,
'Tis blessed not to know;
He holds me with His own right hand,
And will not let me go,
And lulls my troubled soul to rest
In Him who loves me so.

So on I go not knowing,
I would not if I might;
I'd rather walk in the dark with God
Than go alone in the light;
I'd rather walk by faith with Him
Than go alone by sight.

Someday our faith will become actual sight. Our night
will turn into glorious, everlasting day. There will be no sorrow, no change, no disappointments, no darkness, for we will
be in the Lord's presence at last. He alone will be our
source of Eternal Light. His presence will be fully realized
and enjoyed. That will be a day of great rejoicing as we sing
to our greatest source of Light – the Lamb of God.

And the city has no need of sun or moon to shine on
it, for the glory of God gives it light, and its lamp is
the Lamb. And night will be no more.
Revelation 21:23, 22:5.

Until then, my dear sisters, be content and rejoice that you may sing in the shadow of the Lord's glorious presence as you walk through the path of life. You may not know where He will lead, but you can always know that He is with you. Be willing to follow Jesus in sweet surrender. You will find that it is the only way to have true victory in Him.

CHAPTER 6

The Victory of Surrender

I SURRENDER ALL
By Judson W. Van DeVenter

All to Jesus, I surrender;
All to Him I freely give;
I will ever love and trust Him,
In His presence daily live.

Refrain:
I surrender all, I surrender all,
All to Thee, my blessed Savior,
I surrender all.

All to Jesus I surrender;
Humbly at His feet I bow,
Worldly pleasures all forsaken;
Take me, Jesus, take me now.

All to Jesus, I surrender;
Make me, Savior, wholly Thine;
Let me feel the Holy Spirit,
Truly know that Thou art mine.

All to Jesus, I surrender;
Lord, I give myself to Thee;
Fill me with Thy love and power;
Let Thy blessing fall on me.

All to Jesus I surrender;
Now I feel the sacred flame.
O the joy of full salvation!
Glory, glory, to His Name!

Above the serene surface of Silver Lake the mist hovers like a filmy veil. The pine trees stand tall along the opposite shore, sheltering this little world from any outside noise or influence that would disturb the quiet solitude of this place. The morning air seems to quiver with the anticipation of the coming of the rising sun. Everything is still, and waiting, like the expectant silence of an orchestra watching for the conductor's cue. One hardly dares to move a muscle lest it disrupts this rare, delicate peace. Streaks of pinks and orange soon appear in the eastern sky, as the sun begins to rise, dissipating the foggy air to reveal the glassy surface of the lake that reflects the surrounding trees and the pale blue sky above. The world seems wrapped in tranquility, and the scene evokes calmness in the observing soul. Without any forewarning, a subtle, gentle breeze ripples across the placid water, making the reflected sunshine look like dancing diamonds on the crown of the lake's surface. As from the wave of the conductor's baton, the world suddenly comes to life as the watching musicians begin their concert of the lively sounds of living. The trees whisper in the wind, birds chirp, warble, and trill. Dogs begin to bark; cabin doors slam; boat motors roar. It is a beautiful concert of life in its own way, but quite matchless to the exquisite beauty of the former reverence that was known just moments before.

In the hush of God's presence where all is still and no worry ripples across the serene surface of our hearts, we must come to Him surrendered. We cannot come with an agenda of our own.

We must never approach our quiet time with Him as something to just be checked off of our "To Do" list for the day. We do need to cultivate the habit of seeking His face on a regular, daily basis, but we must leave room for spontaneity and freedom. Be willing to leave your "fishing nets" of duty behind on the shore the moment that you hear Jesus calling, "Come, follow Me."

I remember one such spontaneous moment that I recorded awhile back:

"...While I was in the process of doing dishes, I noticed the golden gleam of the setting sun. I just couldn't resist running outside to revel in it. With my apron flapping and my heart light, I ran down the driveway. The western sky was a sweep of gold as the sun gently lowered itself among the emerald green trees in the field beyond the road. It was dazzling. The air had the fresh smell of the recent rain. Everything looked its best – bright and shiny like a new penny. A heron flew high in the sky – a blue jay "cawed." How awesome and beautiful Jesus must be, since all of this is just a creation – a masterpiece of His."

As we come to Jesus each day, let's come with an open heart and hands, emptied of our own wills and our own way. Yield your heart to Jesus and be open to receive direction from Him. To be yielded is to give up our way, our rights, and let Him take the lead as we follow in His way. Unlike our way, His way is perfect.

> *This God — His way is perfect; the Word of the LORD proves true; He is a shield for all those who take refuge in Him. For who is God, but the LORD? And who is a rock, except our God? — the God who equipped me with strength and made my way blameless.* Psalm 18:30-32.

The Spirit cannot fully fill or indwell a heart that is already full. Do not crowd out His sweet presence with anxiety, burdens, plans, conditions, or expectations.

ANXIETY

When we are anxious, it shows a lack of faith and trust in God. Since *"without faith it is impossible to please Him,"* (Hebrews 11:6) there is no room for fretting in God's presence. If circumstances cause us to worry, we must remind ourselves that the only action that we are able to take is to pray.

Do not be anxious about anything, but in everything by prayer and supplication with thanksgiving let your requests be made known to God. And the peace of God, which surpasses all understanding, will guard your hearts and your minds in Christ Jesus.
Philippians 4:6-7.

Worry is not only displeasing to God, it is unproductive and harmful. Worry gets us nowhere, and keeps us from going anywhere.

Anxiety in a man's heart weighs him down, but a good word makes him glad. Proverbs 12:25.

Turn your anxiety into prayer. Let it move you to trust and reliance on the Lord. Our troubles really are blessings in disguise, if we have the eyes of faith to see them that way.

*So we do not lose heart. Though our outer self is wasting away, our inner self is being renewed day by day. **For this light momentary affliction is preparing for us an eternal weight of glory beyond all comparison**, as we look not to the things that are seen but to the things that are unseen. For the things that are seen are transient* [fleeting, passing, brief, temporary, short-lived], *but the things that are unseen are eternal.* II Corinthians 4:16-18.

BURDENS

When we choose to carry our own burdens and cares, refusing to cast them on the Lord, we will grow weary and distant from Jesus. We have the mentality in America that we need to be self-sufficient by "pulling ourselves up by our bootstraps."

I have found that though I want God's help and blessing, I often take my burdens back on my shoulders. This is a very prideful way of thinking, because the Lord has taken full responsibility for His children. Unlike us, He never wears down or gets exhausted. His strength never lags. He wants to daily take our burdens from us and give us rest in His sufficient care.

> *Blessed be the Lord, who daily bears our burden, the God who is our salvation.* Psalm 68:19. NASB

He who carries our burdens for us wants us to follow His example in carrying the burdens of our brothers and sisters in Christ.

> *Bear one another's burdens, and so fulfill the law of Christ.* Galatians 6:2.

We all are in this together – learning to walk along this path of our Christian life. Having burdens and cares are not unique. The enemy wants us to think that we are the only ones who struggle and strain under our heavy loads, making us think that we are isolated in our troubles and that there is no one to understand. Satan will do anything he possibly can to discourage us and keep our eyes on ourselves and our problems, instead of looking to Jesus or thinking of others by carrying one another's burdens.

> *Humble yourselves, therefore, under the mighty hand of God so that at the proper time He may exalt you, **casting all your anxieties on Him, because He cares for you.** Be sober-minded; be watchful. Your adversary the devil prowls around like a roaring lion, seeking someone to devour. Resist him, firm in your faith, knowing that the same kinds of suffering are being experienced by your brotherhood throughout the world. And after you have suffered a little while, the God of all grace, who has called you to His eternal glory in Christ, will Himself restore, confirm, strengthen, and establish you. To Him be the dominion forever and ever. Amen.* I Peter 5:6-11.

Though it may not seem like it, our trials here on earth are temporary. The Lord has much in store for us in the life to come that will far outweigh our brief and momentary troubles. Let us not waste our energy or strength on our troubles. Give them to the only One who can handle and solve our problems. Our only responsibility is to trust our Father.

PLANS

God gives us wisdom to make Godly choices and plans for our lives, but oftentimes we don't consult Him first. If we want God's control and blessing in our lives, we need to come to Him emptied of our own plans and ambitions.

So often we come to God having a blueprint already laid out of what we think our lives should look like. We ask Him to bless and fulfill our plans, but what He desires of us is that we come to Him, with an empty page, open hands, and a willing heart, saying: "make me into what You will." Offer Him the blank sheet of your life for Him to draw up the most wonderful plans. Give Him the pen, and He will write the most glorious story for your life. This doesn't mean that we can't have any plans. The Lord gives us ideas, plans, and desires that He wants to fulfill.

> *Now to Him who is able to do far more abundantly than all that we ask or think, according to the power at work within us, to Him be glory in the church and in Christ Jesus throughout all generations, forever and ever. Amen.* Ephesians 3:20-21.

When we come to Him available and willing, we will find that His plans for us often are desires that He has placed in our hearts already.

One winter recently I was going through a rather discouraging time where I was feeling really uncertain about what I should be doing and was struggling with some health issues. For a couple months I had been wondering what the Lord had in store for me to do, and had actually been quite despondent, as I wasn't sure if the Lord could even use me.

As I was sick and feeling quite useless, the thought came to me like a lightning bolt from the sky, "write a girl's devotional." That was it! Writing a book – now I had a purpose, and it was something I had always dreamed of and desired to do!

Several years before the Lord placed the desire to write a book about devotions for girls on my heart. I had spent a few hours writing down some ideas of topics I could write about, but I was in my first year of Bible School, so I set aside my notebook and my ideas for awhile. During the next several years a variety of events and pursuits filled my days, so I had hardly thought about the possibility of writing a book, or that it was even an option for me.

Yet, God was faithful and guided me to His path of service that He wanted me to follow, although it has been quite a long process and not always easy. The result is the book that you now hold in your hands!

Hudson Taylor said: "God gives the best to those who leave the choice to Him."

This wonderful fact holds true for all areas of life, and this has a wonderful application for young women in their desire to be married and have their own family. Somehow we may think we know what we want in a husband, when we want to be married, and how we should meet that special one. Yet if we want God's best, we must lay aside our "perfect plans" and trust His perfect faithfulness to provide. God has our best in mind, so let's leave the choice up to Him.

Likewise, this is how it should be with our plans in using our quiet time and scheduling our days. Nothing comes into our lives outside of God's sovereign control. He allows interruptions, which actually might be His will for us, instead of our original plan. Offer up your plans to the Lord and trust Him to work out what is best.

Many are the plans in the mind of a man, but it is the purpose of the LORD that will stand. Proverbs 19:21.

CONDITIONS

Have you ever found yourself saying to the Lord, "If You do this for me, then I will do this..." Or maybe you have never verbalized it, but have just thought, "If only I had this" or "if only I looked like that..." Without even realizing it, we may be putting certain conditions on God when we come to Him in prayer.

Humanly, we want our comforts, an easy road to walk, time to pamper ourselves, and to be able to bask in the knowledge that "everything is going my way." Maybe we have been approaching our quiet times with conditions, as if we are the ones who call the shots. We may say, "Lord, I will seek You each day - only if it will be sweet and happy, with blue skies above and soft words spoken."

If this is the case, we are in for disappointment. We soon will learn that the Christian life is not easy and full of happiness and comforts. Sometimes we will have to persevere in seeking Him when He feels distant, or we feel dry spiritually. Sometimes our loving Heavenly Father will have to bring words of correction, rebuke, and discipline.

God has called us to deny ourselves and walk on a straight and narrow road. No, we cannot be swept into the easiness of floating down the main stream of the culture around us – and yes, it will be hard! Things will not go our way. As much as we need God's love, we need His discipline (which is also a sign of His love!)

Jesus wasn't very lenient with people who wanted to follow Him on their own conditions.

> *Jesus replied, "Foxes have holes and birds of the air have nests, but the Son of Man has no place to lay his head." He said to another man, "Follow me." But the man replied, "Lord, first let me go and bury my father." Jesus said to him, "Let the dead bury their own dead, but you go and proclaim the kingdom of God."* Luke 9:58-60.

We must forsake all of our stipulations in order to follow Christ on His terms. Coming to the Lord with conditions and stipulations is like saying, "Here I am, Lord, send me – to Honolulu, Hawaii!" Aren't you glad that God loves us unconditionally? Jesus fulfilled all of His conditions for us. Let us be willing to follow Him unconditionally.

EXPECTATIONS

Now this one is a hard one – expectations – which requires a real balance. It would be ridiculous to say that we must have no expectations when we come to the Lord. The psalmist shows great expectation when he says, *"my soul waits for the Lord more than watchmen for the morning..."* Psalm 130:6.

To quote a line from the filming for a German broadcast of "Anne of Green Gables," Rachel Lynde tersely reproved Anne by saying, "Blessed is he that expects nothing for he shall not be disappointed."

Our goal as Christians is not to shield ourselves from disappointments, but to have our lives aligned with God's will revealed in His Word.

Where do our expectations lie? Sometimes I have found that God asks me to surrender all of my expectations to Him, especially when I come before His presence. Our expectations are to **come** from Him.

> *My soul, wait thou only upon God; for my expectation is from Him.* Psalm 62:5. KJV.

We should not come to the Lord with expectations initially. His ways are so much higher and better than our ways. He will show us what to expect

Before heading off on our annual Mexico missions trip, the President of our Bible School encouraged us as students to surrender all of our expectations for our trip and ministry to the Lord. I took his exhortation to heart, and it was amazing to see that the Lord had great things in store for our team, as well as working in my heart personally.

With an attitude of surrender, I was able to see things from a different perspective. It was as if I was able to sit back and watch God work.

Many times I have approached some special quiet time with the Lord expecting to hear from God or receive a special blessing. Often I find that when I come to Him with an open heart and no expectations on my part, that is when He chooses to bless me and speak to me through His Word.

Expect to let God work, and you will see great things. Expect Him to have complete control of your heart and life, and He will transform you in a way you never thought possible.

Expect good – being pessimistic is a very ungodly trait. Even when we find ourselves in the most dire circumstances, God can work things together for good.

> I believe that I shall look upon the goodness of the LORD in the land of the living! Psalm 27:13.

IN SWEET SUBMISSION

Submission is a very unappealing word these days, a quality greatly opposed and misrepresented in the views of our culture. Yet it is vital that as servants of Christ – bondslaves of Jesus – we learn to embrace and cultivate this characteristic in our lives. Especially as ladies we should be seeking to live out God's order for our lives, which includes submitting to our fathers, or if we are married, to our husbands, and being willing to follow their lead.

Submission requires a broken and surrendered will – one that says, "Lord, Your way is best. I am willing to follow You." We must let Jesus be our Master and Leader, as we learn to be His followers. So, why should we submit to Him? Because God gives grace only to the humble.

> *But He gives more grace. Therefore it says, "God opposes the proud, but gives grace to the humble." Submit yourselves therefore to God.* James 4:6-7.

So, let us be surrendered followers of our dear Lord and Master, Jesus Christ. He will not lead us this far to leave us helpless and alone. With joy He will lead those who look to Him with loving eyes of trust and sweet submission. He will lift up those who humbly cast themselves into His mighty hands. This is the true victory of surender!

CHAPTER 7

Walking With Humility

TRUST AND OBEY
By John H. Sammis

When we walk with the Lord in the light of His Word,
What a glory He sheds on our way!
While we do His good will, He abides with us still,
And with all who will trust and obey.

Refrain:
Trust and obey, for there's no other way
To be happy in Jesus, but to trust and obey.

Not a shadow can rise, not a cloud in the skies,
But His smile quickly drives it away;
Not a doubt or a fear, not a sigh or a tear,
Can abide while we trust and obey.

Not a burden we bear, not a sorrow we share,
But our toil He doth richly repay;
Not a grief or a loss, not a frown or a cross,
But is blessed if we trust and obey.

But we never can prove the delights of His love
Until all on the altar we lay;
For the favor He shows, for the joy He bestows,
Are for them who will trust and obey.

Then in fellowship sweet we will sit at His feet.
Or we'll walk by His side in the way.
What He says we will do, where He sends we will go;
Never fear, only trust and obey.

Springtime was coming to the mountains of North Idaho at last. The sun was shining, and the snow was melting fast. The frozen grip of winter was slowly thawing away from the ice-covered river. It felt good for us kids to be out on a hike with Mom. We crossed the bridge that spanned the flowing Moyie River below. The river that appeared so docile in the summer and fall was now a rushing torrent of white-foaming water, tumbling over the riverbed rocks on its way to the Kootenai River in the little mountain town of Bonners Ferry. The noise was almost deafening, though strangely melodic.

Once we crossed the bridge, my brother, sister, and I were thrilled to discover a mini river flowing along the side of the road in the melting snow. Our mom let us watch its ebb and flow, and even let us play with sticks in the little stream for awhile. The water gurgled as it flowed, etching its way through the snowy banks. Our imaginations were alive as we reveled in playing with "our river." Mom had a hard time getting us to leave our little tributary when it was time to head back to our home. We begged Mom to let us come back to our special little spot sometime...

Though I am grown, I still enjoy walks with my mom. The scenery where we live is now drastically different from where we lived in the mountains. No longer do I tag along, stopping to notice every rock, feather, bug, animal track, or mini-river, but the delight is still there in the ever-changing seasons and landscape before me. Now we live in the rural farmland of central Minnesota. Our walks take us by fields where the meadowlarks are singing, pastures of cows or horses grazing on the lush green grass, and farmhouses set in this homey scene of real country life. The advantage of having wide, open spaces, that we affectionately call "fields" around these parts, is that we get an incredible view of the beautiful sky overhead. The blue sky with fluffy white clouds is inspiring, the sunsets are incredible, and the velvet canopy of a star-studded sky is beyond description. Yet, the main enjoyment in my walks now is found in just being with and talking to my mom, knowing that she cares and is willing to listen to my thoughts, joys, concerns, troubles, and questions. I love to hear her gentle, consistent, wise counsel, which is such a treasure for a young lady to be able to receive.

> *"With what shall I come before the LORD, and bow myself before God on high? Shall I come before Him with burnt offerings, with calves a year old? Will the LORD be pleased with thousands of rams, with ten thousands of rivers of oil? Shall I give my firstborn for my transgression, the fruit of my body for the sin of my soul?" He has told you, O man, what is good; and what does the LORD require of you but to do justice, and to love kindness, and to walk humbly with your God? Micah 6:6-8.*

Sometimes when I need to have quiet-time to think and pray by myself, I go out into our field of poplar trees, or stroll around our cow pasture to have time to walk and talk alone with the Lord. I treasure these solitary walks with Jesus, as I share with Him my cares or joys, pouring out my heart to the One who knows me best. No other person can put my heart in tune like He can.

THE LITTLE CARES
By Elizabeth Barrett Browning

The little cares that fretted me,
I lost them yesterday
Among the fields above the sea,
Among the winds at play;
Among the lowing of the herds,
The rustling of the trees,
Among the singing of the birds,
The humming of the bees.
The foolish fears of what may happen--
I cast them all away
Among the clover-scented grass,
Among the new-mown hay;

Among the husking of the corn
Where drowsy poppies nod,
Where ill thoughts die and good are born,
Out in the fields with God.

Just as some children do not respect and honor their parents, and instead prefer to be "calling the shots," sometimes we do not let the Father lead and walk with us. Our pride says, "I know the way which I want to go. I can do it myself." Then sadly we are left on our own, fumbling about in the darkness, until we are willing to admit our mistakes and humble ourselves once again and return to our Father who knew best all along. The reason I grew to enjoy taking walks was because my mom led the way, was always there, and opened my eyes to the beauty of God's creation around me.

If we want to be walking in the grace of God's presence, if we desire to abide under the smile of His favor, if we want to seek His face during our daily devotions, we must walk like Jesus – allowing His humble life to be lived out in us.

Do nothing from rivalry or conceit, but in humility count others more significant than yourselves. Let each of you look not only to his own interests, but also to the interests of others. Have this mind among yourselves, which is yours in Christ Jesus, who, though He was in the form of God, did not count equality with God a thing to be grasped, but made Himself nothing, taking the form of a servant, being born in the likeness of men. And being found in human form, He humbled Himself by becoming obedient to the point of death, even death on a cross. Therefore God has highly exalted Him and bestowed on Him the name that is above every name, so that at the name of Jesus every knee should bow, in heaven and on earth and under the earth, and every tongue confess that Jesus Christ is Lord, to the glory of God the Father. Philippians 2:3-11.

Before this beautiful passage overwhelms you with the seemingly unattainable model of Christ's perfect humility, take a closer look at the above passage. It tells us that this attitude and mindset **IS** ours in Christ Jesus! It isn't something to make us defeated and be hanging over our heads like an unattainable goal. It is already ours, yet we need to make an effort to appropriate it and live it out in our lives.

Remember this truth – the perfectly humble Savior has exchanged His life for yours when you came to Him in faith trusting His redemption. Your ugly pride and arrogant self was nailed with Jesus to the cross so that His sinless, pure, humble life may be lived out in you. You are a new creature. The high standard of perfection that God requires is met in Christ alone – not in our pitiful self-efforts.

It is a choice we have to make, though. Our attitude doesn't just morph into a right attitude without a conscious decision to let Christ work it in us. We are called to *"put on the Lord Jesus Christ, and make no provision for the flesh, to gratify its desires."* Romans 13:14.

Our dear President Lincoln once said, "Most folks are about as happy as they make their minds up to be." I think that goes for humility, too. We must choose to be humble people. So also, we are as humble as we make up our minds to be.

We can talk about being humble, we can imagine it, painting a lovely picture of what it looks like, but until we put our faith into action we will not be living out a humble life.

> *Clothe yourselves, all of you, with humility toward one another, for "God opposes the proud but gives grace to the humble." Humble yourselves, therefore, under the mighty hand of God so that at the proper time He may exalt you, casting all your anxieties on Him, because He cares for you.* I Peter 5:5-7.

Humility is a beautiful and simple garment that we are required to wear everyday. If we desire a deeper, closer relationship with the Lord Jesus, we must come in humility. God opposes the proud; they cannot stand in His presence, but to the humble He offers His grace and favor to allow them to come near.

We by nature long to be accepted. We want to please and earn favor. Sometimes we place far greater requirements and expectations on ourselves in hopes to secure greater favor from the Lord. Yet, He has no favorites. There is a false humility that looks good from the outside, but on the inside it is just as prideful as a loud, arrogant person.

Outer sacrifice, strict asceticism, poor-little-old-me mentality, gloom and despair – these are not humility. We don't need to be walking timidly, somehow trying to appease the wrath of an angry judge.

> *For this is the love of God, that we keep His commandments. And His commandments are not burdensome.*
> I John 5:3

He doesn't require much from us in comparison to all that He has done for us, other than to be walking in close communion with Him. We simply are to be practicing loving kindness, justice, and to be walking in humility with our God.

It is not to be a picture of a stern master walking alongside his slave ready to whip his back the moment he slows down in his work or steps out of line. It is like a loving Father who walks alongside his small child - protecting, guiding and encouraging him on his way. It is a secure, joyful, trusting relationship as the child learns to look up to his father, trusting him to lead.

A PRIDEFUL HEART

There is a different, more subtle pride that people often don't own up to. I would call it the "pathetic martyr disorder." Under the guise of being "independent" and "self-sufficient" we refuse the Lord's merciful help.

Like Peter who was indignant that Jesus would lower Himself and perform the humblest task of washing his feet, we ourselves sometimes say or just think, "No, Lord, You shouldn't have to clean up after me, patching up my mistakes. I got myself into this one; I'll find my way out."

Self-sufficiency is a terrible aspect of pride. Yet Jesus gently and firmly reminded Peter that He must wash his feet. He is the only One who can make sense out of the tangled web of our lives, so we should surrender our troubled lives to Him in humility.

Self-pity – this is another form of pride that hinders us from being the joyful, victorious followers of Jesus. Sometimes when we are discouraged and our day hasn't been going right or going our way, we'd just rather sink into the cozy comforter of self-pity and gloom rather than giving thanks to the Lord in every situation. Often we want everyone else to join with us in our dirge of discontent. Sometimes we grow accustomed to being downtrodden. We grow used to being lowly, needy people. A downcast heart becomes our way of life. Sometimes it feels rather good to enjoy our little woes and muse over our little wounds. We wallow in our own misery, somehow forgetting that there is more to life than the present.

Self-righteousness, self-condemnation, self-esteem, selfish pursuits, selfish ambition, all of these are forms of pride. Notice the emphasis on self in all of these conditions. As Christians, self must die; it must be brought low, so that we only exalt Christ. He will not share His glory with another.

> *The haughty looks of man shall be brought low, and the lofty pride of men shall be humbled, and the LORD alone will be exalted in that day.* Isaiah 2:11.

BEING LIFTED UP

The One who humbles us and brings us low will also exalt us and lift us up!

> *Humble yourselves, therefore, under the mighty hand of God so that at the proper time He may exalt you...* I Peter 5:6.

It is not for us to exalt ourselves. Yet, don't hang back in
fear and doubt. Reach out to grasp His loving, Almighty
hand that will pull you up out of the miry clay so that you
can place your feet on the Solid Rock.

As God's chosen, adopted children, we are His precious
treasure. Our worth is great in His sight – He was willing to
sacrifice His only Son to redeem us and bring us to Himself.
Mary, the mother of Jesus, is probably the loveliest example
of a woman of true humility. She humbly accepted God's
amazing call on her life. Her beautiful prayer reveals her
heart of humble praise.

> And Mary said, "My soul magnifies the Lord, and my
> spirit rejoices in God my Savior, for He has looked on
> the humble estate of His servant. For behold, from
> now on all generations will call me blessed; for He
> who is mighty has done great things for me, and Holy
> is His name. And His mercy is for those who fear
> Him from generation to generation. He has shown
> strength with His arm; He has scattered the proud in
> the thoughts of their hearts; He has brought down the
> mighty from their thrones and exalted those of hum-
> ble estate; He has filled the hungry with good things,
> and the rich He has sent away empty. He has helped
> His servant Israel, in remembrance of His mercy, as
> He spoke to our fathers, to Abraham and to his off-
> spring forever." Luke 1:46-55.

True humility magnifies God. Turn from looking to yourself or to others, by looking to Christ alone. Draw other
people's eyes to Christ, and not to yourself.

Contentment and humility go hand in hand. Paul shares
with us a precious lesson that he had learned through the
refining fires of life.

> Not that I am speaking of being in need, for I have
> learned in whatever situation I am to be content. I
> know how to be brought low, and I know how to
> abound. In any and every circumstance, I have

learned the secret of facing plenty and hunger, abun-
dance and need. I can do all things through Him
who strengthens me. Philippians 4:11-13.

A dear friend of mine (who now, by God's grace and blessing, is my fiancé) once shared with me about how he has discovered that to the measure which he is willing to be abased or brought low, to that same measure he will abound. That certainly gave me something to think about! How often I "endure" hard times just waiting to get through to a better place, but do I really accept the trials, or the humbling times with contentment? The blessings and exaltation become all the sweeter if I do.

Sometimes I think we need to learn to be silent when we come before the Lord. How our whining and discontentment must weary His patient ears! Psalm 131 is a simple yet profound picture of the attitude of humility.

LORD, my heart is not lifted up; my eyes are not
raised too high; I do not occupy myself with things
too great and too marvelous for me. But I have
calmed and quieted my soul, like a weaned child with
its mother; like a weaned child is my soul within me.
Psalm 131:1-2.

A weaned child is content to just be with his mother, not crying or demanding to be fed. His needs are already satisfied. He quiets his heart and longings, so that he may enjoy the calmness and delight of his mother's presence.

Do you find that there is something still holding you back from walking with the Lord? Maybe there is unforgiveness in your heart. How can we expect to walk with the Lord and receive His forgiveness, if we do not extend it to others? We are greatly loved and lavishly forgiven, so we should be free to love and forgive others.

HUMILITY OF RECEIVING

The incredible thing is not that we love God, but that He loves us. Bask in that love which motivates us to love Him and our neighbors.

What arrogance and ignorance of us to say, "Lord, You have given us Your Son for our salvation, but this trouble of mine, I can handle. I will not impose on Your kindness or generous heart to meet this need."

In other words, we are saying, "I can do it myself. I don't need anything from you, Lord."

God in His mercy and wisdom brings us through situations and trials where we no longer can rely on ourselves. Our weakness and human frailty become once again very apparent, and we, resembling helpless babes, cry out to our Father – depending on Him alone to see us through.

We must be willing to accept guidance. He wants us to be utterly dependent on Him. Don't be afraid to acknowledge your weakness and failings to the Lord, since He already knows. Humility requires honesty and openness. Psalm 25 is a lovely prayer to pray when you are humbly seeking the Lord's guidance.

> *To You, O LORD, I lift up my soul. O my God, in You I trust; let me not be put to shame; let not my enemies exult over me. Indeed, none who wait for You shall be put to shame; they shall be ashamed who are wantonly treacherous. Make me to know Your ways, O LORD; teach me Your paths. Lead me in Your truth and teach me, for You are the God of my salvation; for You I wait all the day long. Good and upright is the LORD; therefore He instructs sinners in the way. He leads the humble in what is right, and teaches the humble His way. Turn to me and be gracious to me, for I am lonely and afflicted. The troubles of my heart are enlarged; bring me out of my distresses. Consider my affliction and my trouble, and forgive all my sins.* Psalm 25:1-5, 8-9, 16-18.

WALKING WITH TRUST AND OBEDIENCE

There is really no way for us to be happy in Jesus if we do not trust and obey Him. Many of our problems in life would be eliminated if we would just follow those two little admonitions – trust and obey.

Trust: having reliance, dependence, and confidence in God; cancels out all fear, worry, and languishing faith.

Obedience requires compliance, submission, respect, conformity to God's commands. It is the opposite of our tendency to be wayward, non-committed, selfish, defiantly doing it our own way, living contrary to God's Word.

Oh, sisters, as we come to Jesus each day, longing to walk closely with our dear Friend, let us not make the common mistake of being a half-surrendered Christian. Give your ALL to be under Christ's control and guidance. It may not happen overnight, but little by little, the Lord will show you areas that you need to entrust to Him. At that point, give it to Him, though you doubt and may not understand. He is faithful and some day faith will become sight. Therefore, walk with Jesus in dependent, humble faith. Draw from His great resources that are readily available. Never be too proud to ask. We have not, because we ask not. Depend completely on God and His Word for your life, strength, and wisdom.

When we learn to walk with the Lord in humility, He will show us wonderful truths from His Word. We will find the Scriptures to be a great source of refreshment as they transform our lives to become more like Christ's.

CHAPTER 8
The Word that Transforms

THE WORD OF GOD
by Haldor Lillenas

The Word of God is like a light
That shines serenely thro' the night;
Its rays will light my weary way
To the realms of a fair, unending day.

Refrain:
The Word of God is strong and sure,
Forevermore it shall endure,
When oceans cease to kiss the shore,
When suns shall set to rise no more;
'Mid crash of worlds it shall remain
Unshaken midst the starry rain,
Upon its firm foundation strong,
I will plant my feet thro' the ages long.

The Word of God is like a sword
That pierces hearts, thus saith the Lord;
And like a hammer, weighty, strong,
That can break up the rocks of sin and wrong.

The Word of God is like the bread
On which the hosts of old were fed;
From Heav'n it came to fill our need,
Hungry hearts it will satisfy indeed.

The Word of God is like a fire,
It kindles in our hearts desire
To see its Author face to face
And to know all the fullness of His grace.

The fresh snow had fallen during the night, transforming the appearance of the surrounding fields and woods. The meadows are laced in a mantle of pure white, as the snow graces every pine bough and tree branch. The thick, downy comforter looks completely new – untouched – unspoiled – undefiled. The ground that was once ugly, brown, and barren, is now completely changed to a sparkling white garment of clean snow.

It would seem that the snow has come to stay, until... drip... drop... Could it possibly be? Without much warning, the snow begins to melt, as the spring rains begin to loosen winter's bitter grasp. The dry, cold soil is soon softened, ready for seed to be planted that will someday become a fruitful crop. The harvest will return blessings a hundredfold to the hand that faithfully and carefully planted and watered it as it grew, resulting in joyful singing.

God's living and active Word can wonderfully transform the lives of those who accept it. Nobody else's words have the capacity to soften our hearts, cleanse us from our sins, give the greatest source of wisdom, or produce abundant fruit in our lives.

Scripture is beautifully likened to rain and snow, both of which have a tremendous cleansing, and thirst-quenching ability, which results in bountiful fruit.

> *For as the heavens are higher than the earth, so are My ways higher than your ways and My thoughts than your thoughts.*
> *For as the rain and the snow come down from heaven and do not return there but water the earth, making it bring forth and sprout, giving seed to the sower and bread to the eater, so shall My word be that goes out from My mouth; it shall not return to Me empty, but it shall accomplish that which I purpose, and shall succeed in the thing for which I sent it.*
> *For you shall go out in joy and be led forth in peace;*

*the mountains and the hills before you shall break
forth into singing, and all the trees of the field shall
clap their hands. Instead of the thorn shall come up
the cypress; instead of the brier shall come up the
myrtle; and it shall make a name for the LORD, an
everlasting sign that shall not be cut off.*
Isaiah 55:9-13.

The Hardened Soil of Our Hearts

Our hearts may grow hardened if we allow other idols in
our lives, such as the deceitfulness of riches to consume our
focus, or if we grow bitter because of the trials that come our
way. Sin also makes our hearts stony as we persist in going
our way. What can be done about the condition of such a
heart? Who can change it?

*And I will give them one heart, and a new spirit I will
put within them. I will remove the heart of stone from
their flesh and give them a heart of flesh, that they
may walk in My statutes and keep My rules and obey
them. And they shall be My people, and I will be
their God. Ezekiel 11:19-20.*

How does He soften the soil of a hard heart? By sending
us His Word. His Word is quick and powerful, judging the
thoughts and attitudes of the heart, not in a cold, harsh way,
but like the warm sunshine that melts the snow and reveals
what is underneath. Sometimes we speak harsh words in
frustration to change people we love, but really this hardens
hearts. Gentle, soft answers turn away wrath and soften
hearts. Sometimes truth is firm, unshakable, and unapolo-
getic. Truth can hurt, but must always be spoken in love.
The Lord sometimes speaks to us in soft, gentle tones, sometimes in unmistakable honesty that cuts to the core, but
always with love.

THE PURE WATER OF GOD'S WORD

Nothing quite quenches our thirst like water. We wouldn't live long if we didn't have any water. God created water for us to drink: yet it also has another special quality: water cleanses things.

> *I am the true vine, and My Father is the vinedresser. Every branch in Me that does not bear fruit He takes away, and every branch that does bear fruit He prunes, that it may bear more fruit. You are clean because of the word that I have spoken to you. Abide in Me, and I in you. As the branch cannot bear fruit by itself, unless it abides in the vine, neither can You, unless you abide in Me.* John 15:1-4.

The Lord has declared us clean already because of the Word that He has spoken to us. The president of my Bible school would say to us students: "Walking in this world our feet get dirty." We need to come frequently to Christ and His Word to be cleansed and sanctified. Let's soak our mind and thoughts in the pure water of God's Word.

Take time to meditate, ponder, dwell, and contemplate, by turning over in your mind the wonderful, transforming truths of God's Word. It is much like a cow chewing on its cud, ruminating the same food over many times to break down its fodder, making it more digestible. When we "ruminate" on God's Word we will glean much more from it than when we quickly gulp it down. We will find much more joy and delight in our heart when we savor God's Words to us each day.

> *Your words were found, and I ate them, and Your words became to me a joy and the delight of my heart, for I am called by Your name, O LORD, God of hosts.* Jeremiah 15:16.

The Scriptures also can be an incredible source of material and inspiration for our prayers. Praying the Psalms can be especially helpful. I remember praying Psalm 25 over many times when I was seeking the Lord's guidance during a specific season in my life. After some time had passed, I was amazed to see how the Lord answered those specific pleas for direction.

Another beautiful aspect of God's Word is that it was given to us, not only to instruct us, but to give us encouragement so that we may have hope in this dark and decaying world. It helps us see beyond the temporal to God's eternal purposes, producing in our lives perseverance and endurance.

> *For whatever was written in former days was written for our instruction, that through endurance and through the encouragement of the Scriptures we might have hope.* Romans 15:4.

We also have been given God's Word as the sword of the Spirit to fight against Satan's attacks. It is the only offensive weapon we have. Jesus Himself used Scriptures when He was tempted.

> *...and take the helmet of salvation, and the sword of the Spirit, which is the Word of God.* Ephesians 6:17.

God's promises are indeed very great, as they allow us to become partakers of the divine nature. Like Christian in "Pilgrim's Progress," we will find that the promises which are offered to us in the Bible are the key to unlock the door to set us free from "the dungeon of despair."

> *His divine power has granted to us all things that pertain to life and godliness, through the knowledge of Him who called us to His own glory and excellence, by which He has granted to us His precious and very great promises, so that through them you may become partakers of the divine nature, having escaped from the corruption that is in the world because of sinful desire.* II Peter 1:3-4.

It is good to have a plan for reading through the Bible, but it is also good to be in tune to the Spirit's leading - to have structure, but also spontaneity. Let the Holy Spirit be your teacher as you study God's Word each day. We want to accurately handle and apply God's Word, not taking bits and pieces to fit to our liking. We should want to honor the whole counsel of God's Word, never disregarding any portion of it.

> *But the Comforter, which is the Holy Ghost, whom the Father will send in My name, He shall teach you all things, and bring all things to your remembrance, whatsoever I have said unto you.* John 14:26.

Sometimes I have learned so much from God's Word when I have followed the Spirit's prompting in what to read. I'll be sitting there reading a certain passage of Scripture or praying about a specific concern. The Holy Spirit then brings another verse to mind that addresses the issue I'm praying or studying about. I've found that sometimes the words of a hymn will come to mind, too. It is as if the Holy Spirit prepared a whole Bible study for me! It is very special to see how the Lord can specifically direct us when we are sensitive to His leading, and that God's Word speaks directly to our current situation. His Word is alive and active in the life of a Christian.

> *For the word of God is quick, and powerful, and sharper than any two edged sword, piercing even to the dividing asunder of soul and spirit, and of the joints and marrow, and is a discerner of the thoughts and intents of the heart.* Hebrews 4:12

I have learned that I need to be faithful in reading the Word despite my feelings, or even if the "heavens remain silent." Perseverance and faith are two important qualities that God wants to develop in our lives, as we faithfully read His Word. Whether we discover profound truths or simple promises that we already knew, we will grow in character.

We need to be careful that we do not read into certain Bible verses or apply things to our life that were meant for a specific person or time in history. We must be careful not to take not take verses out of context to apply them to our situation. Ask God to give you wisdom and guidance in reading and applying His Word. He is pleased to answer that prayer, as God longs to protect His Word.

Our faith and walk with Jesus will grow cold and distant, if we don't nourish our souls with the heavenly manna of God's Word each day. It is our treasure and greatest supply of spiritual nourishment.

I have not departed from the commandment of His lips; I have treasured the words of His mouth more than my portion of food. Job 23:12.

A STOREHOUSE OF WISDOM

Sometimes the rain comes in torrents, abundantly filling the lakes, rivers, and streams to overflowing. The desert is transformed to an exotic oasis. Everyone's thirst has been quenched and their cup is running over with God's abundant provision.

I was surprised one day when my supervisor at the nursing home where I worked commented on the fact that I had more "common sense" than some of the other recreation leaders, who were twice my age and had much more experience. I had often felt intimidated by them because of my age, inexperience, lack of training, and degrees. Then I realized that those things don't amount to much if one hasn't been trained and disciplined by God's Word – the true source of wisdom.

Don't let your Bible reading be an end in itself. We read God's Word to know more about the Word – Jesus Christ. We don't just cling to and memorize the written Word, we cling to the Living Word who is dwelling in us. Jesus Himself is the source of all wisdom and knowledge.

That their hearts might be comforted, being knit together in love, and unto all riches of the full assurance of understanding, to the acknowledgement of the mystery of God, and of the Father, and of Christ; in whom are hid all the treasures of wisdom and knowledge. Colossians 2:2-3.KJV.

God's Word is to be shared with others and is profitable for training, reproof, and correction. It is so important to commit Scripture to memory, especially while you are young, so that it may richly dwell in your mind and heart wherever you are and in whatever you are doing.

Let the Word of Christ dwell in you richly, teaching and admonishing one another in all wisdom, singing psalms and hymns and spiritual songs, with thankfulness in your hearts to God. Colossians 3:16.

Memorizing Scripture is very important, but it doesn't matter what quantity you have memorized, if you are not putting it to practice. Knowing the Bible shouldn't just result in head knowledge, but should actually be applied and lived out in our lives.

Do not become little Scribes and Pharisees, who knew the Scriptures so well, yet did not believe in the real Word of Life whom they actually saw with their very own eyes. Our eternal life isn't found only in God's Word; it is found in the living person of Jesus Christ!

*You search the Scriptures because you think that in them you have eternal life; and it is they that bear witness about Me, yet you refuse to **come to Me** that you may have life.* John 5:39-40.

Let's become so familiar with Scripture, that it just flows out in our words of advice to others, in our prayers, in our letters, affecting all that we say and do.

One of the things that really impressed me about the writings of A. W. Tozer is that although he rarely referenced Bible verses, his books were saturated with God's Word. One could easily recognize the thoughts and verses that he had in mind while he was writing.

God's Word can speak directly to us. Sometimes the Holy Spirit illumines specific verses that we can apply directly to our circumstances, but we need to be very careful not to take verses out of context and the original intent of the author.

THE GOOD NEWS

So much in our lives is temporary. How much time and effort we put into things that will not last! Our minds are so often filled with thoughts of earthly things that will fade away.

> *For "All flesh is like grass and all its glory like the flower of grass. The grass withers, and the flower falls, but the word of the Lord remains forever." And this word is the good news that was preached to you.* I Peter 1:24-25.

God's Word is eternal and will remain forever. The news these days is so disheartening and discouraging, but God's Word is meant to lift us up – it is good news of great joy.

> *As cold waters to a thirsty soul, so is good news from a far country.* Proverbs 25:25. KJV

What happy uplifting people we would be if our hearts and minds were filled with God's good news of Jesus Christ! We in turn are to bring this good news to the world.

> *How beautiful are the feet of them that preach the gospel of peace, and bring glad tidings of good things!* Romans 10:15.

OUR DAILY BREAD

The Scriptures are our very source of life and strength as a believer, without which our faith could not survive. The Lord will provide refreshment for our weary souls just as He did for the Israelites so long ago.

> *And He humbled you and let you hunger and fed you with manna, which you did not know, nor did your fathers know, that He might make you know that man does not live by bread alone, but man lives by every word that comes from the mouth of the LORD.*
> Deuteronomy 8:3.

As good as devotionals are – nothing can compare to God's Word. There is no other book that can give encouragement, conviction, hope, life, and joy like the Bible.

Get in the habit of taking only your Bible (maybe a hymnal, too) when you go to have some quiet time with the Lord. God does use the words of His servants today, but **His** Word is what transforms lives.

The words that I write in this book will some day pass away, but God's Words will never pass away. It may seem ironic for me to say this as I write my book, but I feel that if all this book accomplishes is to point you to Jesus and His Word, I have not written it in vain.

Let me encourage you to take your Bible out to read every morning. The Israelite children gathered their daily supply of manna each morning. Morning by morning, you can nourish your spirit and soul, with the wholesome bread of God's Word.

CHAPTER 9

Morning by Morning

GREAT IS THY FAITHFULNESS
By Thomas O. Chisholm

Great is Thy faithfulness, O God my Father;
There is no shadow of turning with Thee;
Thou changest not, Thy compassions, they fail not;
As Thou hast been, Thou forever will be.

Refrain:
Great is Thy faithfulness!
Great is Thy faithfulness!
Morning by morning new mercies I see.
All I have needed Thy hand hath provided;
Great is Thy faithfulness, Lord, unto me!

Summer and winter and springtime and harvest,
Sun, moon and stars in their courses above
Join with all nature in manifold witness
To Thy great faithfulness, mercy and love.

Pardon for sin and a peace that endureth
Thine own dear presence to cheer and to guide;
Strength for today and bright hope for tomorrow,
Blessings all mine, with ten thousand beside!

Morning by morning the sun never fails to rise. With consistent regularity it makes its appearance each day, whether it is a sunny day, or it is hiding behind the clouds. During the summer months the sun rises very early – when most of us are still in bed. During the winter it may seem that the sun hardly appears for those who have to leave for work early in the morning and come home when it is quite late. Yet, one of the few things that we can know for certain in this world is that the sun will never fail to rise.

God's Word gives us the wonderful assurance: *"while the earth remains, seedtime and harvest, cold and heat, summer and winter, day and night, shall not cease."* Genesis 8:22.

This promise made thousands of years ago has never been broken, and will hold true until this earth passes away.

There is something so comforting in familiar things. That is what makes home so precious. I remember after our family had moved to our big, old farmhouse, I was surprised how I missed the familiarity of our old house. We were so happy to leave the busy street and the smaller house where we used to live and finally be able to move out into the beautiful farmland of Pine City, Minnesota, yet I still missed the familiar surroundings of the home my family had previously lived in for ten years. Our new place did seem quite homey, though, and sometimes it felt as if we had lived there for a long time. As we busied ourselves with the necessary work of fixing up this old farm, the place seemed to become like our own. Slowly, without always realizing it, our country home has now become very familiar and dear to our hearts, as we have laughed, prayed, worked, and cried together here!

Lately I have been realizing the beauty of my regular, morning meetings with my Savior. It has been a routine since I was quite young to spend the first moments of every day reading God's Word and praying. It is something that I have observed my parents and older sister do faithfully every day. There is no better source for feeding our souls than the nourishing bread of God's Word.

But He answered, "It is written, 'Man shall not live by bread alone, but by every word that comes from the mouth of God.'" Matthew 4:4.

Sometimes my quiet-time with the Lord is short; sometimes I could spend more than an hour. Some days I come to Jesus all out of sorts, with my day looming before me like an endless tunnel with so much to accomplish. There have been days that I don't feel well, or feel dry spiritually. Yet, there are other days when I come eagerly into God's presence, hungering for His Words of righteousness. Sometimes I come rejoicing in who He is and in what the Lord has done for me. Yet, through it all, I keep coming.

This rare consistency in my life is so comforting. We all long for stability in our life one way or another. Some changes are good, yet some changes we go through are hard to accept and adjust to. Time takes its toll on our lives, our health, and even on our outward "beauty." Gray hairs appear and the frailty of life soon becomes very apparent. Beautiful clothes wear out. Loved ones pass away. Favorite pets die. History has shown the rise and fall of many empires throughout the ages. Landscapes can change in a day, as a tornado or flood wipes out trees and landmarks that have stood for hundreds of years.

As for man, his days are as grass: as a flower of the field, so he flourisheth. For the wind passeth over it, and it is gone; and the place thereof shall know it no more. Psalm 103:15-16. KJV

Not much in this life is lasting or unchanging. That is why I think the unchanging nature of God is so incredible, but also hard for us to humanly comprehend.

Of old You laid the foundation of the earth, and the heavens are the work of Your hands. They will perish, but You will remain; they will all wear out like a garment. You will change them like a robe, and they will pass away, but You are the same, and Your years have no end. The children of Your servants shall dwell secure; their offspring shall be established before You. Psalm 102:25-28.

Yes, changes are good and I know that God wants our lives to be new and different from our old way of life before we knew Jesus as our Savior, but it isn't so much that He wants to change us. He doesn't say "I'm going to change you, Teresa, so that you will become a better Teresa." No, He rather exchanges me for His Son. He says, "I'm going to exchange Teresa with My Son, Jesus. It will be no longer her, but Him living through her."

FAMILIARITY

There is a danger in common use or casual regard. There is great joy in knowing someone really well, but often we see more and more of people's faults the more we get to know them – things that are not apparent to the casual acquaintance. With the Lord it is different. The more we get to know Him, the more of His perfection we see. We never want to let our years of walking with the Lord make us grow casual or complacent in our relationship with Him. We mustn't become familiar with the Lord in a way that would bring about a lack of respect for Him. Christ is so highly exalted above us. Yet, He is willing to walk with those who are humble in heart.

I have heard it said so often that we should never be comfortable with where we are in our Christian life. There is always a need for growing and changing. This is true, yet I tend to see it a little differently. As we have put on Christ Jesus as Savior, as we have put off the old, sinful nature, and have put on the new life in Christ, we should grow accustomed and comfortable to the familiar "surroundings" of life with Him, walking in His presence along the paths He leads us in. We want Him to be well-known in our lives, to be recognizable. We want our moments spent with Him to be frequent, regular, and well established. We can then learn to rest, as expressed by the title of one of Bill and Gloria Gaither's songs: "Feeling at Home in the Presence of Jesus."

One of the key ways to feel at home in Christ's presence is to remain faithful in seeking the Lord regularly. Make it a habit and pattern every day to seek Him in the morning. Especially if we are busy, it will be crucial that we have time set aside to seek Him. It won't just happen. We have to persevere and press on to know the Lord.

> *Let us know, let us press on to know the LORD; His going out is sure as the dawn; He will come to us as the showers, as the spring rains that water the earth."*
> *What shall I do with you, O Ephraim? What shall I do with you, O Judah? Your love is like a morning cloud, like the dew that goes early away."*
> Hosea 6:3-4.

For the how, when, and where we meet Jesus, we can ask the Lord to show us, but let's do our part and just come. We have nothing to lose, and everything to gain. He will meet us there.

When I was talking with my grandpa on the phone one day in the winter, he reminded me in his cheery voice that "it won't be long until it is spring!" In the middle of a long, cold Minnesota winter, that promise sure seems like gold! My grandpa has lived through 92 winters and he knows that without fail, spring will come again. There is always that hope, that assurance, that peaceful confidence that spring WILL come again.

As surely as we expect spring each year, we can expect the Lord to meet with us, when we seek to know Him and read His Word each day. May our love be stronger than the morning mist that soon evaporates with the heat of the day. Our love will show its strength when we persevere in meeting with the Lord daily, when we persevere in continuing to seek Him, pressing on to know the Lord.

God wants to produce the beautiful fruit of faithfulness in our lives. This may show through our continuity, constancy, and consistency in seeking the Lord each day. I praise God that He remains faithful to me at all times, no matter what I've done. How I long to mirror His faithfulness in my own life! He wants to work in us His faithfulness and reliable, unchanging character.

> *Every good gift and every perfect gift is from above,*
> *coming down from the Father of lights with whom*
> *there is no variation or shadow due to change.*
> James 1:17.

THE BEAUTY OF THE MORNING

Some people naturally enjoy the morning, while others do not, but whether you do well in the morning or not, it is so crucial to start your day in God's presence by having His perspective and help as you face the tasks of the day. It is very important to keep Jesus first in your life by spending time with Him each day. Granted, there will be days when events arise that we may have to rearrange our schedules and routines. Yet, the fact is that if we don't take time to spend with the Lord first, we may not get around to it the rest of the day.

When I was younger I would start reading the Bible as soon as I woke up, even before I got out of bed, but now I find it is helpful to at least get somewhat ready for the day, so that I'll be more alert and focused for a quality time with Jesus.

The first subject that we usually started out our homeschool day with was our family Bible-time. If there were days that we couldn't get a lot of our schoolwork done, we at least tried to have our Bible-time together. This was an excellent way to instill in our young lives the centrality and importance of Scripture – above academics, good grades, or any human knowledge. The encouraging thing is that as we learn more of God's wisdom from His Word, He helps us grow in our "academic knowledge" as well!

Morning by morning, month after month, year after year, keep seeking the Lord. Gradually it will become a habit. Eventually it will become a necessity, so that you cannot get through the day without your regular morning meetings with Jesus. Ultimately it will be the source of your daily bread and the most treasured moments in your day.

> *The steadfast love of the LORD never ceases; His mercies never come to an end; they are new every morning; great is Your faithfulness. "The LORD is my portion," says my soul, "therefore I will hope in Him."*
> *The LORD is good to those who wait for Him, to the soul who seeks Him. It is good that one should wait quietly for the salvation of the LORD.*
> Lamentations 3:22-26.

My grandma would tell her children how she would offer her day up to Jesus, and also how important it is to nurture one's faith – even more important than feeding our physical bodies. Grandma's faith was lived out each day in loving expressions to her family. She showered her ten children and many grandchildren with consistent, faithful love – treating each one equally, yet relating to each uniquely.

Of anyone that I've ever known, my grandma's life was like a lovely building, not ostentatious, but like a home that is warm, welcoming, familiar, comfortable, bright and clean.

You are God's field, God's building. According to the grace of God given to me, like a skilled master builder I laid a foundation, and someone else is building upon it. For no one can lay a foundation other than that which is laid, which is Jesus Christ. Now if anyone builds on the foundation with gold, silver, precious stones, wood, hay, straw – each one's work will become manifest, for the Day will disclose it, because it will be revealed by fire, and the fire will test what sort of work each one has done. If the work that anyone has built on the foundation survives, he will receive a reward. If anyone's work is burned up, he will suffer loss, though he himself will be saved, but only as through fire.

Do you not know that you are God's temple and that God's Spirit dwells in you? If anyone destroys God's temple, God will destroy him. For God's temple is holy, and you are that temple. I Corinthians 3:10-17.

We shouldn't grow complacent in daily routine, but instead we should remember that just as day by day, brick by brick, the magnificent cathedrals were built, so our faith must be fed to grow day by day, piece by piece. Then we will become a beautiful sanctuary where God's spirit dwells, learning to abide in Him amidst the mundane work of everyday life.

CHAPTER 10

Abiding Amidst the Mundane

DAY BY DAY

By Karolina Sandell-Berg;
translated by Andrew L. Skoog

Day by day and with each passing moment,
Strength I find to meet my trials here;
Trusting in my Father's wise bestowment,
I've no cause for worry or for fear.
He whose heart is kind beyond all measure
Gives unto each day what He deems best -
Lovingly its part of pain and pleasure,
Mingling toil with peace and rest.

Every day the Lord Himself is near me
With a special mercy for each hour;
All my cares He fain would bear, and cheer me,
He whose name is Counselor and Power.
The protection of His child and treasure
Is a charge that on Himself He laid;
"As your days, your strength shall be in measure,"
This the pledge to me He made.

Help me then in every tribulation
So to trust Thy promises, O Lord,
That I lose not faith's sweet consolation
Offered me within Thy holy Word.
Help me, Lord, when toil and trouble meeting,
Ever to take, as from a Father's hand,
One by one the days the moments fleeting,
Till I reach the promised land.

It was another day of work for the young shepherd boy, David. He had learned to work hard from a very early age as he tried to catch up with his brothers while they cared for their father's sheep. Now the responsibility of caring for the flock lay solely on his young, but capable shoulders. Though being a shepherd was not the most praised career, David learned to enjoy his work, and found it gave him a wonderful opportunity to turn his heart to his God. Numerous songs and prayers were written as David kept watch over his sheep under the starry sky. How he marveled at the myriad of sparkling stars in the dark canopy of the sky above him each night! Before sunrise each morning, he awakened the glorious dawn with the joyful sound of his voice and harp as he praised the Lord. David often enjoyed watching the fluffy lambs play in the springtime with the fresh green grass and new flowers growing all around. While resting in the green pastures by the quiet lake, David basked in the warm sunshine, as the Lord restored his soul with sweet peace.

Sometimes I feel that the very routine and mundane things of life could make me worn out and draw me away from the Lord, but God never intended that our walk with Him be one of devout seclusion. He does call us to step aside from the busyness of life, yet it is so vital for young ladies who are in training for the high calling of motherhood to learn the value of abiding in Christ amidst the mundane chores of everyday life.

"Among the green pastures of unfolded clothes
Amid the still water of dish suds and foam,
I find restoration that I would never have known,
Outside of this place I lovingly call 'Home.'"[17]

Invite Jesus into your kitchen as you wash the dishes or bake some cookies for your younger siblings. He really is interested in your daily cares and offers His presence "to cheer and to guide."

The Lord is my shepherd, I shall not want. He
maketh me to lie down in green pastures: He leadeth
me beside the still waters. He restoreth my soul: He
leadeth me in the paths of righteousness for His
name's sake. Yea, though I walk through the valley of
the shadow of death, I will fear no evil: for Thou art
with me: Thy rod and Thy staff they comfort me.
Thou preparest a table before me in the presence of
mine enemies: Thou anointest my head with oil; my
cup runneth over. Surely goodness and mercy shall
follow me all the days of my life: and I will dwell in
the house of the Lord for ever. Psalm 23. KJV

Psalm 23 is a beautiful picture of the Lord's personal
shepherding in our lives. Its verses inspire pastoral scenes of
green meadows flocked with white, wooly lambs and crystal
clear lakes that reflect the luminous sky above. While poetry
may seem lofty and unrealistic, it really is just simple, practical truths written in exalted language.

Poetry is the music of the soul, and the Lord Himself is to
be our song, He often uses music and poetry to reach our
hearts when simple words of prose could not.

Somehow our spirit yearns for beauty and poetry amidst
the monotony and dreariness that can settle on our daily life.

Our family's dear friend, Denise Nickel, once commented,
"I just long to soak in His presence when I need to be soak-
ing my hands in the dishwater."

How often I have lingered in the Lord's presence, not
wanting to leave my morning quiet time with Him to face
the challenges of the day ahead or to tackle the mundane
tasks set before me. The Lord knows our weakness, so He
offers His strength afresh to us each day.

...as thy days, so shall thy strength be.
Deuteronomy 33:25. KJV

Like the dear, old monk, Brother Andrew, we can be practicing the presence of God while going about our daily chores. My grandma would often remind her children to "take up your cross daily."

Somehow the quiet peace and satisfaction of being in Jesus' presence alone, which hovers around our spirit like the morning mist, often evaporates when we face the warm sun and the heat of everyday trials.

Lest we lose heart, let us turn to Jesus. He has promised His enduring presence to help us through the course of our day. Focusing on this knowledge can transform how we look at our daily, mundane chores.

He who has formed us has given us the tasks before us each day. Invite Jesus to share in every care and burden of your daily life. As beautiful as our solitary moments with Him are – our daily walk with him can be just as lovely. He designed us to care and labor for what He has placed in our lives.

Most of Jesus' life here on earth was spent working as a carpenter. He is well acquainted with the toil of earthly work. Yet, we also know that Jesus was in close communion with His Father.

God created and cherishes our natural, physical lives, as well as our spiritual lives! Our communion and time spent alone with Him is of great value, but it doesn't somehow elevate us above the common things of life.

What gain has the worker from his toil? I have seen the business that God has given to the children of man to be busy with. He has made everything beautiful in its time. Also, He has put eternity into man's heart, yet so that he cannot find out what God has done from the beginning to the end. I perceived that there is nothing better for them than to be joyful and to do good as long as they live; also that everyone should eat and drink and take pleasure in all his toil—this is God's gift to man. I perceived that whatever God does endures forever; nothing can be added to it, nor anything taken from it. God has done it, so that people fear before Him. Ecclesiastes 3:9-14.

We often like to think about that solitary verse, *"He has made everything beautiful in its time,"* yet have we ever considered the context? Could it be that the Lord intends to make our "business" and our "toil" beautiful in its time? Can we possibly find joy and beauty in the normal, everyday work that is before us? God's gift to us is to take pleasure in our toil. It is never fulfilling or satisfying to be constantly doing a job that you hate or feel unfit for.

It is God who giveth us richly all things to enjoy.
I Timothy 6:17. KJV

As young ladies it will be imperative to cultivate a grateful attitude for the work that the Lord gives us each day. We can learn to abide in Christ amidst the mundane drudgery of work and household chores. We will find the sweet satisfaction of doing our jobs well as we walk in close fellowship with Him day by day.

CHRIST AND YOUR KITCHEN
Author Unknown

Will Christ come to your kitchen
When you're busy there all day?
Can you feel Him sitting with you
In a homey sort of way?

You may be washing dishes,
Or deep in batter or dough;
Your face all flushed and smeary
But He'll not mind you know.

For Jesus was a working man,
And labored with His hands
So take Him to your kitchen
For He freely understands.

Will Christ come to your kitchen
Or will you bid Him rest
Within the comfort laden lounge
As suits an honored – Guest?
And will you entertain Him
With every luxury there
But ban Him from your inmost thoughts
And each housewifely care?

Yet Jesus was a working man
Who gladly did His part:
And when we share with Him the toil
We're nearest to His heart.[18]

His Presence is Our Provision

For the trials and cares we face, our deliverance and help
is found in the true Word of God. For every need and prayer
we have – Jesus is the ultimate answer.

> *"Fear not, for I have redeemed you; I have called*
> *you by name, you are Mine. When you pass though*
> *the waters, I will be with you; and through the rivers,*
> *they shall not overwhelm you; when you walk through*
> *the fire you shall not be burned, and the flame shall*
> *not consume you. For I am the Lord your God, the*
> *Holy One of Israel, your Savior."* Isaiah 43:1-3.

The flame of persecution and misunderstanding shall not
consume us. The rivers of suffering and care will not over-
whelm us. The fire of trials and temptation will not burn us,
because we are His; He is with us and He is the Lord our
God – our Savior.

It is good to have a plan for how to read God's Word, but
often the real strength for our day is found when we lay our
daily needs before Jesus and find that He has supplied ample
provision for them in His Word – and in Himself.

ABIDING IN CHRIST WHILE YOU WORK

I am the vine; you are the branches. Whoever abides in Me and I in him, he it is that bears much fruit, for apart from Me you can do nothing. John 15:5.

Consider a grapevine. The main vine that all of the branches grow out of is thick and solid. You can even swing on a grapevine! Its roots are secure, and through the vine flows the life giving nutrients for the branches to bear fruit. If you take a look at the branches that stem from the vine, you will find pencil thin sticks — nothing much to them. Yet these branches can be heavy laden with ripe, juicy grapes. The branches are just the channels. It would be silly to look at a grapevine and give all the credit to the flimsy little branches for the beautiful clusters of grapes that are produced. It is the vine that is important. The vine is the source and gives the branches strength to bear the fruit. Take a branch off of the vine, and it cannot bear fruit by itself. It will just wither and die!

So it is with us. Apart from Jesus, we can do nothing. Any good that we try to do in our own strength and effort, apart from the Lord Jesus, will just shrivel and be of no value. If we want to have a fruitful life in Christ, we need to abide in Him. Abiding in the Lord means to dwell, rest, or remain in Him. It is to take up residency in Him. It is not a position that we need to strive to attain. As a child of God's, we are in Christ. Abiding in Him is a position that we can claim daily by faith. Not only do we abide in Christ for our life and strength, He abides in us. He exchanges our life for His. Our life He has crucified, so that He may live His life through us.

> *I have been crucified with Christ. It is no longer I who live, but Christ who lives in me. And the life I now live in the flesh I live by faith in the Son of God, who loved me and gave Himself for me.*
> Galatians 2:20.

The Lord doesn't want us to compartmentalize our lives in such a way that leaves Him out of our everyday work. He wants our hearts to be focused on Him as our hands are busy.

"My Father God, help me to expect Thee on the ordinary road. I do not ask for sensational happenings. Commune with me through ordinary work and duty. Be my Companion when I take the common journey. Let the humble life be transfigured by Thy presence. Some Christians think they must be always up to the mounts of extraordinary joy and revelation; this is not after God's method. Those spiritual visits to high places, and that wonderful intercourse with the unseen world, are not in the promises; the daily life of communion is. And it is enough. We shall have the exceptional revelation if it be right for us. There were but three disciples allowed to see the Transfiguration, and those three entered the gloom of Gethsemane. No one can stay on the mount of privilege. There are duties in the valley. Christ found His life-work, not in the glory, but in the valley and was there truly and fully the Messiah. The value of the vision and glory is but their gift of fitness for work and endurance."[19]

As we walk with Jesus in our daily life and work, His very presence will make our work a joy. Let us persevere in our daily work here on earth, as it won't be long before we are heading to our heavenly home. Our toil and labor here will be exchanged for the glorious rest of heaven. It wasn't long before David, the hardworking shepherd boy, went from working in the pasture to becoming a king in the palace.

Now we have need to learn the perseverance and patience of working and waiting for the Lord. The refreshment of Christ will come to us like streams in the dry, thirsty desert.

CHAPTER 11
Like Streams in the Desert

REVIVE THE HEARTS OF ALL
By James M. Black

God is here, and that to bless us
With the Spirit's quickening power;
See, the cloud already bending,
Waits to drop the grateful shower.

Refrain
Let it come, O Lord, we pray Thee,
Let the shower of blessing fall;
We are waiting, we are waiting,
Oh, revive the hearts of all.

God is here! We feel His presence
In this consecrated place;
But we need the soul refreshing
Of His free, unbounded grace.

God is here! Oh, then, believing,
Bring to Him our one desire,
That His love may now be kindled,
Till its flame each heart inspire.

Savior, grant the prayer we offer,
While in simple faith we bow,
From the windows of Thy mercy
Pour us out a blessing now.

The dry, arid desert stretches out to the horizon where the hot, red sun is finally setting after the scorching heat of the day. The sky shimmers, liquid-like, as the heat waves rise from the sun-scorched sand. The landscape is barren of anything green or living. Just the dry sand ripples and scatters in the hot wind. Rain hasn't been seen for months. The cloudless sky seems to mock the helpless ground below, as it mercilessly holds back its storehouse of rain. Weary, parched travelers are almost ready to faint as their thirst drives them on to find a source of water somewhere, anywhere. Their joy knows no bounds when they discover a water supply. A bucket plunged into the depths of the well comes up brimming with cold, clear water to quench the thirst of the exhausted sojourners.

One of the toughest enemies we may face, when we are first learning to seek God daily is when we feel dry spiritually. Like the dry ground, sometimes our dry, thirsty spirits cry out, "Send forth the rain - the fresh water of Your Word!" I am so thankful to the Lord that He provided complete atonement, so that the status of my relationship with Him is not measured by my feelings, which vary every day like the ever-changing appearance of the sky – some days sunny, some days full of storm clouds.

Sometimes our spiritual life seems like a desert: deserted... dry... lifeless. The words desert and deserted both speak of lonely, empty, forsaken places. The Lord Jesus promised to never forsake us, so we must remember and cling to that promise, even if our feelings tell us otherwise. Though God does not intend to leave us there, sometimes He lets us go through these times. When we are feeling dry, lacking in spiritual fervor, freshness, and enthusiasm, we should never become discouraged and desire to give up on seeking the Lord. It is probably the most crucial time to be seeking Him! Do not look to yourself and think that you must have messed up somewhere, or that you must try to find your way out of the "desert" on your own. It is good to ask the Father to show us if there is sin in our life that may have hardened our heart or dried up our affections for Him, but we don't want to get caught up in self-introspection.

> "It is good for us to look at self and know how loathsome it is, but with one look at self we must take ten looks at Christ..." 20

Sometimes the doubts may come as to whether you are really a Christian, when you are feeling dry or dull spiritually. **How Satan loves to use this lie!** He often tries to keep us down when we are feeling down. Don't listen to him! Our salvation is not based on our feelings. It is only through the blood of Jesus that we are saved. Our faith in Him is what will bring us through a doubting time.

Even great men and women of the faith have gone through dry times in their lives as they have faithfully walked with the Lord. I also have gone through some tough times spiritually, especially when I was struggling with depression for a few years. By God's grace I never gave up reading His word nearly every day. Looking back, I can now see that God's hand was guiding my steps toward Him in a very loving way. Many seeds were being planted in the barrenness of my soul during that time that only came to fruition in later years. Sometimes the Lord brings us low to teach us more about His humility and our unworthiness, so that when He lifts us up, we may rejoice with pure joy.

> *The LORD is good to those who wait for Him, to the soul who seeks Him. It is good that one should wait quietly for the salvation of the LORD. It is good for a man that he bear the yoke in his youth. Let him sit alone in silence when it is laid on him; let him put his mouth in the dust— there may yet be hope; let him give his cheek to the one who strikes, and let him be filled with insults. For the Lord will not cast off forever, but, though He cause grief, He will have com-*

passion according to the abundance of His steadfast love; for He does not willingly afflict or grieve the children of men. Lamentations 3:25-33

After several years of going through a depression, the Lord brought me to a place of glorious freedom and joy in Him I had never known before. I do believe that I had a few "glimpses" of heaven, and because of that experience, the vision for this book was formed.

THE TWO RESPONSES

The book of Ecclesiastes gives us a real picture of depression as experienced by those in the world. When Solomon was depressed, he turned to other things for fulfillment, as he relied on his own wisdom.

> *I searched with my heart how to cheer my body with wine—my heart still guiding me with wisdom—and how to lay hold on folly, till I might see what was good for the children of man to do under heaven during the few days of their life... So I became great and surpassed all who were before me in Jerusalem. Also my wisdom remained with me. And whatever my eyes desired I did not keep from them. I kept my heart from no pleasure, for my heart found pleasure in all my toil, and this was my reward for all my toil. Then I considered all that my hands had done and the toil I had expended in doing it, and behold, all was vanity and a striving after wind, and there was nothing to be gained under the sun.* Ecclesiastes 2:3, 9-11.

In contrast when David was depressed, he cried out to God in true honesty. The Psalms are a wonderful source of comfort and help for those who are struggling with discouragement as David often did. We can learn much from the response of this man after God's own heart.

Why are you cast down, O my soul, and why are you in turmoil within me? Hope in God; for I shall again praise Him, my salvation and my God. Psalm 42:11.

We have much to praise and thank the Lord for. Our response to discouraging circumstances and feelings should be trust, faith, and grateful reliance on the Lord. We are extremely rich in Him. We need to focus on what we have, not on what we don't have!

THE FATHER'S RESOURCES

In the parable of the prodigal son, we learn a very important lesson from the example of the eldest son.

Now his older son was in the field, and as he came and drew near to the house, he heard music and dancing. And he called one of the servants and asked what these things meant. And he said to him, "Your brother has come, and your father has killed the fattened calf, because he has received him back safe and sound." But he was angry and refused to go in. His father came out and entreated him, but he answered his father, "Look, these many years I have served you, and I never disobeyed your command, yet you never gave me a young goat, that I might celebrate with my friends. But when this son of yours came, who has devoured your property with prostitutes, you killed the fattened calf for him!" Luke 15:25-30.

The proud, elder son was always with his father, but he never made use of the resources that were readily available to him. What a bitter, selfish, joyless person that older son must have been. He felt keen indignation, maybe even hurt that his rebellious brother was being treated like a king, while his own faithfulness was seemingly overlooked by his father. Yet this son may be similar to many Christians today.

More and more, I have come to see that the older son's attitude mirrors what I have sometimes felt myself. Having been raised in a Christian home, and knowing about Jesus ever since I was little has been one of the greatest blessings in my life, yet I have seen how easy it is to allow spiritual pride to creep in unknowingly.

Notice in the parable that the older son reminds his father that he had served him, and he never disobeyed. Do you ever find yourself expecting a fanfare for something you've done? We all long to be recognized. It can be quite upsetting to us when our faithful hard work is overlooked and someone else who is "undeserving" gets all the praise.

Outwardly the older son did all the right things – he never disobeyed his father's commands, but inwardly he was just as rebellious as the prodigal. The father reached out and went to his stubborn son, seeking to reconcile both his children.

Let's keep in mind the context of this passage: Jesus was telling these parables to the Pharisees who were grumbling that Jesus was eating with "sinners." Their legalism had hardened their hearts from showing any love or compassion to others.

The Pharisees' observance of God's law was not the problem; it was their heart condition that grieved Jesus. All of our good deeds and righteous living will amount to nothing, if our heart is not right with God.

> *Woe to you, scribes and Pharisees, hypocrites! For you are like whitewashed tombs, which outwardly appear beautiful, but within are full of dead people's bones and all uncleanness. So you also outwardly appear righteous to others, but within you are full of hypocrisy and lawlessness.* Matthew 23:27-28.

There is a tendency among Christians to be overly concerned with legalism. "Don't be pharisaical," someone may tell you if you are holding to higher standards than others.

In the Bible we are exhorted to live lives that are worthy of the Lord, and to please Him in all things, but it must come from the heart. Jesus wants to change us from the inside out.

Before we despair, let us take a closer look at the father's incredible response to his oldest son. There is no harshness in the father's response. (I think the father's response is actually the climax of this passage, which shows us the heart of our Heavenly Father.)

When the proud son had refused to come into the banquet hall – out of his pride and simmering anger - the father came out to him and earnestly entreated his son to come in and rejoice over the return of his wayward son. The father's love is so wide – wide enough to embrace both sons, the prodigal and the proud.

In tones probably husky with emotion, the father gently, yet firmly, tells his firstborn:

> *"Son, you are always with me, and all that is mine is yours. It was fitting to celebrate and be glad, for this your brother was dead, and is alive; he was lost, and is found."* Luke 15:31-32.

The father puts the focus back on himself and not on the son's service. Our former pastor, Dean Paulson, had mentioned that the wonderful, amazing, unbelievably good news is not how much we love God – what we can do for Him - but how much He loves us – what the Lord has done for us!

The story ends unfinished and leaves us wondering: was the heart of the proud son ever softened? Did he end up going into the banquet hall after all, quietly approaching his younger brother and clapping his hand on his shoulder, saying, "Welcome home, kid?"

We'll never know, but I think Jesus left His hearers hanging there for a reason. The choice was up to them – the Pharisees – and now to us today. How will we respond to the words of the Father? Will we let go of our stubborn pride and self-righteousness and rejoice over sinners who repent? Or will we refuse to make use of the Lord's resources so readily available to us?

The Lord may be speaking similar words to us, "Daughter, don't you see? All of My resources are readily available to you. What is Mine is also yours. If you want to celebrate, joy is yours for the asking. You are always with Me. Isn't that enough to satisfy?"

Why do we as children of the great, all-powerful God, walk around as if we are poor beggars always looking for more? Do we need joy? God's storehouse is always full! Do we lack faith? Ask God and He will give us more. Are we dry spiritually? The Lord will pour out His refreshing restoration. May the words of our loving Father continue to echo in our minds: *You are always with Me, and all that is Mine is yours.*

WALK BY FAITH

In Bible Doctrine class at the Bible school I attended, Pastor Dave Jore showed us a good illustration for the order of our Christian life. Like a train, the *facts* of our faith are the engine; they must come first. We believe in Jesus' precious atonement, which is a solid fact – an unchanging truth. Next comes our *faith*. We have never actually seen Jesus, or witnessed His death for ourselves, but through faith we believe and know that it is so, no matter what our feelings may tell us. Then our feelings may follow our faith, just like the caboose. The train can run without the caboose, so we can trust and know that we are saved, no matter what our feelings tell us. If we let our *feelings* take the lead, we are in for a wild ride! Yet feelings are a very real, necessary part of life and should not be disregarded. We are so intricately made that we could never separate our feelings from our faith. It is important though to keep our feelings in proper perspective, which will be crucial when we seek the Lord in our quiet time each day.

Sorrow and joy – we all experience these common emotions throughout our lives in differing measures. It may seem like a paradox that we can be both sad and happy at the same time.

As sorrowful, yet always rejoicing...
II Corinthians 6:10. KJV

In Mrs. Cowman's devotional, Streams in the Desert, there is a lovely allegory that describes Sorrow and Joy as if these qualities were real people. The beauty of each is quite unique, as their positions are so vastly different. Yet, they were grieved when they realize that they can never be united - until, they saw the King. As they kneeled before Him they said:

> "I see Him as the King of Joy," whispered Sorrow, "for on His head are many crowns, and the nailprints in His hands and feet are the scars of a great victory. Before Him all my sorrow is melting away into deathless love and gladness, and I give myself to Him forever."
> "Nay, Sorrow," said Joy softly, "but I see Him as the King of Sorrow, and the crown on His head is a crown of thorns, and the nailprints in His hands and feet are the scars of great agony. I, too, give myself to Him forever, for sorrow with Him must be sweeter than any joy that I have known." [21]

After discovering that sweet knowledge, Sorrow and Joy then could see that in their King they were indeed one. Only Christ can unite joy and sorrow in such a beautiful, tender way.

It is true that as followers of Christ, when we are sorrowing in this world, we also may be rejoicing in Him. In our quiet-times we may find this true as well. Though we feel dry, we must continue on in faith, for we know that the Lord will daily renew our spirits.

So we do not lose heart. Though our outer self is wasting away, our inner self is being renewed day by day. For this light momentary affliction is preparing for us an eternal weight of glory beyond all comparison, as we look not to the things that are seen but to the things that are unseen. For the things that are seen are transient, but the things that are unseen are eternal. II Corinthians 4:16-18.

THE WATERS OF REFRESHMENT

Though one cannot tell, from what first meets the eye underneath the barren, dry desert there is an incredible source of water just waiting to be discovered and put to use. Once the huge water source is tapped into, the wasteland can be transformed into lush, fertile crop land, bringing forth an abundant harvest.

> *Strengthen the weak hands, and make firm the feeble knees. Say to those who have an anxious heart, "be strong; fear not! Behold, your God will come with vengeance, with the recompense of God. He will come and save you." Then the eyes of the blind shall be opened, and the ears of the deaf unstopped; then shall the lame leap like a deer, and the tongue of the mute sing for joy. **For the waters break forth in the wilderness, and streams in the desert; the burning sand become a pool, and the thirsty ground springs of water**; in the haunt of jackals, where they lie down, the grass shall become reeds and rushes.*
> Isaiah 35:3-7

Remember that when you are feeling dry spiritually, and your soul is longing to be refreshed, the Lord has a rich supply of the water of life, readily available to us if we only are willing to ask Him. We can be sure that He will hear us and will supply what we lack.

On the last day of the feast, the great day, Jesus stood up and cried out, "If anyone thirsts, let him come to Me and drink. Whoever believes in Me, as the Scripture has said, 'Out of his heart will flow rivers of living water.'" John 7:37-38.

Under the barren surface of our hearts there is a spring of joy waiting to burst forth. There are great resources at our disposal just waiting to be tapped into. We shouldn't want to hoard this supply to ourselves, but to share it with others, telling them of the great fountain of life that we have found in Christ alone.

With joy you will draw water from the wells of salvation. And you will say in that day: "Give thanks to the LORD, call upon His name, make known His deeds among the peoples, proclaim that His name is exalted." Isaiah 12:3-4.

When the Lord supplies our needs and refreshes our spirits, we will receive wonderful peace from Him. Our hearts and longings will be stilled and satisfied. When our spirits are truly calm and serene, we will be able to reflect the Lord's beautiful image to those around us.

CHAPTER 12

Reflecting His Image

O TO BE LIKE THEE!
By Thomas O. Chisholm

O to be like Thee! blessed Redeemer,
This is my constant longing and prayer;
Gladly I'll forfeit all of earth's treasures,
Jesus, Thy perfect likeness to wear.

Refrain:
O to be like Thee! O to be like Thee,
Blessed Redeemer, pure as Thou art;
Come in Thy sweetness, come in Thy fullness;
Stamp Thine own image deep on my heart.

O to be like Thee! full of compassion,
Loving, forgiving, tender and kind,
Helping the helpless, cheering the fainting,
Seeking the wandering sinners to find.

O to be like Thee! lowly in spirit,
Holy and harmless, patient and brave;
Meekly enduring cruel reproaches,
Willing to suffer, others to save.

O to be like Thee! Lord, I am coming
Now to receive the anointing divine;
All that I am and have I am bringing,
Lord, from this moment all shall be Thine.

O to be like Thee! while I am pleading,
Pour out Thy Spirit, fill with Thy love;
Make me a temple meet for Thy dwelling,
Fit for a life which Thou wouldst approve.

It is a starlit night with the full moon shining brightly down upon the sleeping world. In the dark hush and dewy air, the moonlight traces subdued patterns on the lawn, as it is filtered through the lacy tree branches. On the glassy lake a moon path shimmers on the dark waters. It is a beautiful, peaceful sight. Though the moon is lovely, it isn't like the full brilliance of the sun. The moon actually has no light of its own, only that which it reflects from the sun.

Just like the moon, we too have no light to offer this dark and depraved world other than the light of the Son reflected in our lives. The dictionary gives a good, simple definition of what it means to reflect:

> "To throw back light..."
> "To consider attentively..."[22]

This truth holds a very precious application for our quiet times with the Lord. It is in these times that we can set aside our tasks and come away to a quiet, still place to listen and talk to Jesus, reflecting on Him and contemplating His character. We can "consider attentively" who Jesus is and what His Word says. In so doing, we will begin to "throw back" and reflect His light in our contact with other people.

A SHINING FACE

Let's travel back a moment to Mt. Sinai where the Israelites were encamped while Moses received God's commandments for His chosen people. Moses had the rare privilege of being able to talk with the Lord God face to face.

> *"Thus the Lord used to speak to Moses face to face, as a man speaks to his friend."* Exodus 33:11.

Moses, having beheld God's glory, reflected His light. Moses' close relationship with the Lord did not go unnoticed. It so drastically changed him and left an unmistakable mark that all Israel saw it, yet Moses himself didn't even realize it!

Sometimes we do not know how God is working in our lives to impact the lives of others. We cannot always tell when He is shining through us.

> *When Moses came down from Mt. Sinai... Moses did not know that the skin of his face shone because he had been talking with God. Aaron and all the people of Israel saw Moses, and behold, the skin of his face shone, and they were afraid to come near him.*
> Exodus 34:29-30

Moses' face radiated so brightly that he would wear a veil to cover his face, except when he went into the tent to speak with the Lord.

> *Now if the ministry of death, carved in letters on stone, came with such glory that the Israelites could not even gaze at Moses' face because of its glory, which was being brought to an end, will not the ministry of the Spirit have even more glory? Since we have such a hope, we are very bold, not like Moses, who would put a veil over his face so that the Israelites might not gaze at the outcome of what was being brought to an end. But their minds were hardened. For to this day, when they read the old covenant, that same veil remains uplifted, because only through Christ is it taken away. Yes, to this day whenever Moses is read a veil lies over their heart. But when one turns to the Lord, the veil is removed. Now the Lord is Spirit, and where the Spirit of the Lord is, there is freedom. And we all, with unveiled face, beholding the glory of the Lord are being transformed into the same image from one degree of glory to another. For this comes from the Lord who is the Spirit.*
> II Corinthians 3:7-8, 12-18.

Through Jesus, a way has been provided for us to approach God's throne at any time. God has accepted us through His Son, Jesus, and He even calls us "friends."

REFLECTING

What does it mean exactly to be reflecting God's image? When our lives are a clean and purified surface, we will be able to reflect and throw back the light that the Lord shines on us from His Word and from His radiant face. When we get a picture of the Lord in all of His goodness and beauty, and as we read His Word, we will want to become like Him, desiring to reflect that same light to others.

Wouldn't you love to hear someone say to you, "Whenever I am with you, I feel like I am with Jesus?"

God knew our human limitations and how we need people. Sometimes I have thought that if Jesus is my all in all, I should not need other people, but oh how I love to actually **see** Christ's loving look, **feel** His strong hand, and **hear** His gentle and encouraging words through those that He has brought into my life. He uses these people to show me more of who He is.

Let Jesus have your hands and heart to show His care and love to this hurting world. People really are hungering and longing to see a glimpse of what God is truly like in us. It should be our desire to be a reflection that would point them to Him.

How do we reflect Christ to those around us? Imitate Him!

> *Therefore be imitators of God, as beloved children.*
> *And walk in love, as Christ loved us and gave*
> *Himself up for us, a fragrant offering and sacrifice to*
> *God.* Ephesians 5:1-2.

It is always so cute to see little toddlers imitating their parents. As they play with a pretend telephone they often capture their mom's "telephone voice." Children, out of respect and love, often want to be "just like Mommy" or "just like Daddy" when they grow up. In their play, girls pretend to keep house and care for babies like their mothers, and little boys just love to pretend to go to work like Dad.

God wants us to be like that, desiring to follow His example. His beloved, cherished children, how could we not help but want to be just like Him?

Yet, as we desire to become mature and "grow up" in our faith, we must take a step further and realize that the Christian life isn't just a life of imitation, it is a life that appropriates Christ's life and righteousness, which has been imparted to us. To imitate is to copy someone. To appropriate is to take what belongs to someone else and use it for yourself. God desires that we take Christ's life that was given to us and appropriate His righteousness as our very own.

> *For our sake He made Him to be sin who knew no sin, so that in Him we might become the righteousness of God.* II Corinthians 5:21.

When we grasp this truth and let this sweet realization sink into our hearts and minds, our lives will be full of joy as we rejoice in our hope of glory; which is Christ living in us. (Colossians 1:27.)

REFLECT GOD'S LOVE!

The chief characteristic that we should reflect from God is LOVE. Christ loved to the point of death.

> *Beloved, let us love one another, for love is from God, and whoever loves has been born of God and knows God. Anyone who does not love does not know God, because God is love. In this the love of God was made manifest among us, that God sent His only Son into the world, so that we might live through Him.* I John 4:7-9.

Jesus gave Himself willingly on our behalf. Can we not do the same everyday for those we love? Give of your time, your money, your interest, your service, and your very life. Without love we are nothing, empty, void of anything useful for blessing those around us.

"If I...have not love, I am nothing."
I Corinthians 13:2.

If we don't love our fellow brothers and sisters in Christ, what will the world think of us? They certainly will not be able to recognize that we are God's children.

By this all people will know that you are my disciples, if you have love for one another. John 13:35.

Our prayer should be that the Lord would make our hearts clean so that we can clearly reflect Him and His love. Another important attribute for us to reflect is God's forgiveness. As we see God's forgiveness for us, who so desperately need it, let us also extend our forgiveness to others.

Take time to consider the character of God. The first and foremost way that we observe God's character, is through His Word. It shows us what is important to Him and who He wants us to become by putting off our old, sinful nature and putting on our new nature in Christ.

Put off your old self, which belongs to your former manner of life and is corrupt through deceitful desires, and to be renewed in the spirit of your minds, and to put on the new self, created after the likeness of God in true righteousness and holiness.
Ephesians 4:22-24.

Christ is our brother and it is the Father's desire that we become like His firstborn. It is quite amazing to see how younger siblings like to copy and unconsciously follow their older sibling's example. As an older sister, I have come to realize that I need to be very careful of how I act and of the things I say, as my younger brothers and sisters easily follow the pattern of how I live before them as they are always watching. God's purpose for us is that we become like Christ:

> *For those whom He foreknew He also predestined to be conformed to the image of His Son, in order that He might be the firstborn among many brothers.* Romans 8:29.

A CLEAR REFLECTION

If we want to reflect His image, we must be still – yielded in His presence; then our lives will clearly represent Christ in this dark world. If our lives are harried and busy all of the time, if our minds are always stressed out and anxious, and if our spirit does not know the deep rest of a heart that is trusting and resting in Christ, we will not be able to clearly reflect Christ. This is just like the surface of a lake that is rippled by the wind, so that it distorts the reflection of the trees on the shore surrounding it.

If we truly desire to be a clear reflection of Christ, we also must be emptied of ourselves. We cannot be building up our self-esteem or seek to have a better image of ourselves. It may seem ironic, but the people who are the most secure in themselves are those who have died to self and are secure in God's love. When we know that God accepts us, we can then accept ourselves. When Christ alone is on the throne of our hearts, there is such peace and harmony in our lives that we would never want self to rule again.

Be willing to humbly ask the Lord to show you any sin in your life that is marring His pure reflection. In confessing and forsaking our sins we will receive His mercy and forgiveness as the blood of Christ purifies and cleanses us of all sin.

Spend much time alone with the Lord in prayer and in

reading His Word. Take time to listen to the gentle voice of the Spirit. My family can often tell which one of my friends I have been spending time with by my mannerisms and tone of voice! I so easily imitate those I'm with, without even realizing it sometimes!

When we spend time with Jesus and walk in close communion with Him throughout the day, people will see Jesus in us. When we look to Jesus, our countenance will even be changed!

> *Those who look to Him are radiant, and their faces shall never be ashamed.* Psalm 34:5.

Let's make it our prayer that the Lord Jesus would stamp His own image deep on our hearts, so that we can become a radiant reflection of Him to the watching world around us. Our lives will then be filled with the fragrant beauty that only comes from living a life of loving devotion to Christ.

CHAPTER 13

The Fragrant Beauty of Devotion

SWEET FRAGRANCE
By Anne Fuller

She loved Him; she worshipped Him.
She gave what she had; she gave what she could,
So He would know she'd mourn for Him
And her worshipful love would never grow dim.

Sweet Fragrance, her precious perfume
Ran down His head, His side
And filled all the room and love was there.

She wept for Him, anointing Him,
Knowing it was for His death soon to come.
Her tears flowed down, mingled the oil,
Knowing it was for His burial.

They took Him, they mocked Him, they beat Him.
Our Savior's side was riven
And as Mary's perfume mingled with His blood,
He smelled the sweet ointment and remembered her love.

Sweet fragrance, His precious blood,
Ran down His head, His side, on Calvary.
Forsaken, alone, He died on the tree,
But for her fragrance.

Sweet fragrance, have you any to give?
Give Him your life, a sweet sacrifice,
And pour out your life for Him.
A sweet fragrance…[23]

In our field beyond the cow pasture is a little grove of wild plum trees. The short, scraggly looking trees seem old and worn out, but their blossoms and fruit are a delight to the one who happens upon their treasures. Wild plum blossoms – their spring-time fragrance is so heavenly. A sweet scent from the delicate, lacy white flowers wafts on the gentle breezes. It is a very pleasing aroma – an aroma that causes one to breathe deeply and smile with pleasure and satisfaction.

Aroma. Scent. Fragrance. It is amazing how something so subtle and unseen can be so noticeable and linger so long. Familiar smells often bring associations to mind. The sweet and spicy smell of apple pies baking may cause us to think of the fall-time in general or we may remember a specific event from our past, such as when we helped our mother peel the fresh apples for the anticipated dessert one crisp autumn day.

Although we aren't always aware of the fact, we ourselves smell like the things we are around. Our family loves to have quesadillas that we fry in olive oil. After stepping out of the house for awhile, it is amazing how noticeable the smell of fried quesadillas is upon entering the house, not to mention that we all smell like quesadillas ourselves!

As daughters of the King, our lives should have a beautiful fragrance – not of ourselves – but of the knowledge of Christ. As we "associate" – spend time with Jesus – our lives will begin to take on His aroma. Although people won't actually tell us that we "smell" like Jesus, they will be able to tell that we have been with Jesus. When we are with others we want them to feel as if they are with Jesus, by the way we talk, act, and live.

But thanks be to God, who in Christ always leads us in triumphal procession, and through us spreads the fragrance of the knowledge of Him everywhere. For we are the aroma of Christ to God among those who

*are being saved and among those who are perishing,
to one a fragrance from death to death, to the other a
fragrance from life to life. Who is sufficient for these
things? Not that we are sufficient in ourselves to
claim anything as coming from us, but our sufficiency
is from God...* II Corinthians 2:14-16, 3:5.

Ultimately we are to be the aroma of Christ **to God** in this
dying world. We aren't first and foremost here to be the fragrance of Christ to the lost world... This thought gave me
real pause to think. We are here to be the aroma of Christ to
God! Our relationship with Him is of the greatest importance – that is why Jesus came to save us, so that we might
have a right relationship with the Father and that we may be
a pleasing aroma in Christ **to God**. We ultimately are
responsible for our own relationship with the Lord - and not
even that - it is by God's grace and Christ's work alone that
we are able to "associate" with Him at all.

When our lives are very focused and intentionally directed
to pleasing the Lord, others will be affected for Christ. God
has made us to be the aroma of Christ amidst a dying world.
As we are "spilling out" our lives in loving devotion to
Christ, the result will be a fragrance that is spread by God
everywhere. He will then shape our hearts to be willing to
love, and then we can pour out our lives to bring this good
news to others.

When we really know and love God, we will have more
of His love for others. It won't be a selfish love or a pres-
sured love. It will be a love that motivates and causes us to
give of ourselves for the sake of others – that they too might
know this Savior and so become a sweet fragrance for Him.

> *Six days before the Passover, Jesus therefore came to
> Bethany, where Lazarus was, whom Jesus had raised
> from the dead. So they gave a dinner for Him there.
> Martha served, and Lazarus was one of those reclin-
> ing with Him at the table. Mary therefore took a*

155

*pound of expensive ointment made from pure nard,
and anointed the feet of Jesus and wiped His feet with
her hair. The house was filled with the fragrance of
the perfume. But Judas Iscariot, one of His disciples
(he who was about to betray him), said, "Why was
this ointment not sold for three hundred denarii and
given to the poor?" He said this, not because he
cared about the poor, but because he was a thief, and
having charge of the moneybag he used to help himself to what was put into it. Jesus said, "Leave her
alone, so that she may keep it for the day of My burial. For the poor you always have with you, but you
do not always have Me."* John 12:1-8.

The first time we hear of Mary, she is sitting at the feet of
Jesus, listening to His teaching. Once again Mary is found
at Jesus' feet. This time out of her deep devotion and love
for Him, Mary offered a costly sacrifice by anointing
Christ's feet with valuable ointment. The house was filled
with the fragrant knowledge of her costly and loving deed.
Yet not everyone approved. Judas in his sly, self-righteous
way, rebuked Mary's extravagant gesture of love. Jesus
made it clear that Mary had her priorities in order. She knew
that Jesus wouldn't always be with her – so she gave abundantly and lavishly while she could. She showed her devotion to Jesus in a very tangible way.

DEVOTION
Often we call our morning quiet times that we spend with
the Lord, "devotions." It is a term so familiar, but when we
look at its full definition, it takes on a whole deeper mean-
ing. According to the dictionary, devotion is:

"The state of being dedicated, consecrated, or
solemnly set apart for a particular purpose."
"A solemn attention to the Supreme Being [God] in
worship; a yielding of the heart and affections to

156

God, with reverence, faith, and piety, in religious duties, particularly in prayer and meditation."
"Ardent love or affection; attachment manifested by constant attention."[24]

So, our devotions are to be a time that we set aside to give our attention, dedication, and affection to God through prayer and meditation on His Word. It is not just something to reserve for one moment of the day, but it is to be a life-long pursuit of giving our "constant attention" and "yielding of the heart and affections to God." It is a "state of being" – a relationship maintained by **being** dedicated, consecrated, and solemnly set apart for the **specific** purpose of knowing, loving, and serving our gracious Lord and Savior.

During their courtship, my brother-in-law, Josh, showed his devotion to my sister, Melissa, in many different ways. Our house is located in the country about an hour north of where Josh's family lives, so Josh literally went the "extra mile" to spend time and do special things with Melissa. They also would spend hours talking on the phone. Josh would send Melissa beautiful bouquets of flowers and enjoyed taking her out to eat. It was very evident that Josh was intentionally devoted and dedicated to Melissa. He was set apart from forming close relationships with other people to give his sole attention to Melissa.

This is what the Lord wants from us, our loving devotion and willingness to be set apart for Him and to be eager to give Him our undivided devotion. It will be costly. It may even make others feel self-reproached by seeing our devotion. Some people may feel slighted.

It is a choice that we have to make for ourselves. The choices that we make now will help set the pattern for the way we will live the rest of our lives. As single young ladies, it is a crucial decision for how we spend our time and who we are being devoted to. Will we be devoted to ourselves, friends, boys, career, or to our wonderful Savior and friend, Jesus Christ?

*There is difference also between a wife and a virgin.
The unmarried woman careth for the things of the
Lord, that she may be holy both in body and in spirit:
but she that is married careth for the things of the
world, how she may please her husband.*
I Corinthians 7:34. KJV.

This verse is not implying that marriage is not to be
desired or is less holy than being single. It is given as a
wonderful reminder of how our single years can be spent for
fruitful service to the Lord, and not wasted on ourselves –
worrying if we are attractive enough, if we are popular, etc.

David gave his son, Solomon, wise advice when he
encouraged him to:

*"...know the God of your father and serve Him with a
whole heart* [undivided devotion] *and with a willing
mind, for the LORD searches all hearts and understands every plan and thought. If you seek Him, He
will be found by you, but if you forsake Him, He will
cast you off forever."* I Chronicles 28:9.

THE SECRET REWARD

When our lives are focused on the Lord, giving Him our
undivided devotion, others will begin to notice the sweet fragrance of the knowledge of Jesus when they are with us.
Our vertical, heavenward focus will result in blessings hori-
zontally, to those around us.

It is wonderful to pray to God along with fellow
Christians, but it is more valuable to pray to God in secret,
when no one else is watching us. It may feel lonely and
solitary at times to be spending so much time alone in secret
with Jesus, but we will be surprised at the results, the
rewards, and what we will reap from having plenty of time
set aside to seek the Lord's face. Others (not ourselves) will
be the first to notice as Christ's light radiates and reflects in
our countenance.

"And when you pray, you must not be like the hypocrites. For they love to stand and pray in the synagogues and at the street corners, that they may be seen by others. Truly, I say to you, they have received their reward. But when you pray, go into your room and shut the door and pray to your Father who is in secret. And your Father who sees in secret will reward you." Matthew 6:5-6.

There is strength in solitude. When we align our heart and lives to God's Word, and when we seek the Lord's face in the quietness, we receive a strength from Him that cannot be shaken. We grow in confidence in the Lord the more we confide in Him alone.

> *For thus saith the Lord GOD, the Holy One of Israel; In returning and rest shall ye be saved; in quietness and in confidence shall be your strength...*
> Isaiah 30:15. KJV.

An incredible thing to think about is that the Lord Himself confides in us. How marvelous that the Mighty, Awesome Creator of the universe is willing to be our friend, and even confides in us, yet He doesn't confide in just anyone. The Lord gives His secret counsel to those who fear, honor, respect, and seek to please Him.

> *The friendship* (secret counsel) *of the LORD is for those who fear Him, and He makes known to them His covenant.* Psalm 25:14.

> Another version says: *"The LORD confides in those who fear Him..."* NIV.

The Lord wants to be our intimate friend. We don't share our secrets with people we pass on the street. We prefer to confide in those we know and love; those who are close and will remain faithful to us.

Let us go to the shelter of God's presence each day, telling Him our troubles, and receiving His loving counsel.

A Pleasing Aroma

In the Old Testament practice of offering animal sacrifices to the Lord, there was a pleasing aroma that was often noted.

>...And the priest shall burn all of it on the altar, as a burnt offering, a food offering with a pleasing aroma to the LORD. Leviticus 1:9.

Yet, under the new covenant, no longer do we need to offer burnt sacrifices to the Lord.

>And every priest stands daily at his service, offering repeatedly the same sacrifices, which can never take away sins. But when Christ had offered for all time a single sacrifice for sins, He sat down at the right hand of God, waiting from that time until His enemies should be made a footstool for His feet. For by a single offering He has perfected for all time those who are being sanctified. Hebrews 10:11-14.

This is an amazing thing, yet hard to comprehend – we are perfected in Christ for all time as we are being sanctified in Him. His sacrifice was enough. It was a perfect, pleasing aroma. It was complete – it is finished! We no longer have to offer sacrifices to gain God's acceptance or approval. The cross of Christ secured that for us.

>And by that will, we have been sanctified through the offering of the body of Jesus Christ once for all. Hebrews 10:10.

Because of Christ's all-sufficient sacrifice for us, each of us in turn must sacrifice our life to God. We must be very careful not to get things turned around and begin to rely on our own "sacrifices" to secure our salvation. As a result of Christ redeeming and purchasing us from sin and death to become one of God's cherished children, we in turn should voluntarily offer up our very lives to Him as our Lord, as well as our Savior.

> *I appeal to you therefore, brothers, by the mercies of God, to present your bodies as a living sacrifice, holy and acceptable to God, which is your spiritual worship. Do not be conformed to this world, but be transformed by the renewal of your mind, that by testing you may discern what is the will of God, what is good and acceptable and perfect.* Romans 12:1-2.

We are called to offer our bodies – our very lives and personalities – to God as a living sacrifice, which will be a pleasing aroma to our King.

PAYING THE PRICE

Mary's sacrificial offering of anointing Jesus with very expensive ointment was an aroma pleasing to Him, because it was offered voluntarily out of a heart of love. Something is not a sacrifice if it costs us nothing!

How much are we willing to give or pay to know and love the Lord in a close, intimate way? Are we willing to spend time in secret with Jesus? We may disappoint a few people or have to say no to some things as a result. How much fun, entertainment, popularity, and adventure are we willing to forfeit for the sake of knowing and pleasing Christ? Is the price too high to pay?

We wouldn't want to be reprimanded like Judas was. Yes, the poor were always with them, but Christ was soon leaving this world. Let us get our priorities right and not miss the opportunity to love and serve Jesus during this short and fleeting life, not rejecting the poor, nor letting our service supersede our relationship with the Lord.

So much of our life can be spent on self-preservation.

Society applauds selfishness. Dieting, beauty magazines, and extensive exercise – everyone seems to be shouting, "Take care of yourself or who else will?!?"

We are to take care of ourselves for the glory of God, but this life isn't all there is – thank God for that!

Remember that, "Only one life, 'twill soon be past... Only what's done for Christ will last!"[25]

When we give of ourselves to Jesus, we may feel "spent", but we have been given great eternal, unseen riches in Jesus.

> "Go, labor on: spend and be spent,
> Thy joy to do the Father's will:
> Is the way the Master went;
> Should not the servant tread it still?"[26]

Let us heed Christ's voice and take to heart the fact that we only have one life to live for Him. May our life be one of beautiful devotion to Jesus Christ – a sweet fragrance unto God! The result will be a fruitful harvest of peace for us that will glorify our Lord and Savior, Jesus Christ.

ABUNDANT BLOSSOMS

Therefore, beloved, since you are waiting for these, [the new heavens and the new earth] *be diligent to be found by Him without spot or blemish, and at peace. And count the patience of our Lord as salvation, just as our beloved brother Paul also wrote to you according to the wisdom given him, as he does in all his letters when he speaks in them of these matters. There are some things in them that are hard to understand, which the ignorant and unstable twist to their own destruction, as they do the other Scriptures. You therefore, beloved, knowing this beforehand, take care that you are not carried away with the error of lawless people and lose your own stability. But grow in the grace and knowledge of our Lord and Savior Jesus Christ. To Him be the glory both now and to the day of eternity. Amen.* II Peter 3:14-18.

It is my prayer that from the pages of this little book you have found encouragement and inspiration, my dear sisters in Christ, to read God's Word and seek the Lord's presence each day. It is an exciting journey, and well worth the effort to follow our Savior as He leads and guides our way. It will not be easy, and you will not always be happy. It is a struggle, as the enemy wants to keep us from spending time with the Lord. I am sure Satan is aware of the incredible transformation that results from dwelling in the Lord's holy presence of light, and of the renewing of our minds that occur when we read and submit to the authority of God's Word.

Don't let the **defeated** foe keep you from living a life of victory as you pursue a closer relationship with the Lord. Just keep in mind that the soldiers closest to the Captain are the ones who are most frequently shot at. There will be discouragements, distractions, and difficulties that you will face, but take heart! The Lord Jesus Christ has overcome this world and all that hinders us from walking in close fellowship with our God and Father.

I encourage you to persevere in seeking the Lord each day and to be willing to learn from your mistakes. Be faithful and don't give up! There will be a fruitful harvest for those who persevere to the end.

> *And let us not grow weary of doing good, for in due season we will reap, if we do not give up.*
> Galatians 6:9.

The rewards will be great as we seek to love the Lord with our undivided devotion. He will place in us the desire to seek and obey Him above any other. The Father will take our broken lives that we offer to Him and make them whole. He will take our sorrow and give us Christ's deep joy. He will take our discontent and unrest and give us the sweetest peace of mind and contentment that we have ever known. Most importantly, Jesus will fill our heart's deepest need to love and be loved, by enabling us to love others as He does, and will also encourage our hearts with the sweet assurance of God's steadfast love for us.

In your quiet time, sow generously, and you will be amazed at the bountiful harvest of fruit that you will reap. The rewards are not only evident in this life; they will continue to bear fruit in the next.

> *The point is this: whoever sows sparingly will also reap sparingly, and whoever sows bountifully will also reap bountifully. He who supplies seed to the sower and bread for food will supply and multiply your seed for sowing and increase the harvest of your righteousness. You will be enriched in every way to be generous in every way, which through us will produce thanksgiving to God.*
> II Corinthians 9:6, 10-11.

Jesus will not leave you helpless as you desire to seek

Him. He has seen fit to provide all that you need from His abundant resources. As you spend much time with the Lord, you will come to see how faithful and willing He is to meet your every need – though it will be in His way and in His timing.

So, dear sisters, may you continue to "grow in the grace and knowledge of our Lord and Savior Jesus Christ," in such a way that He will ultimately receive all of the glory as your life begins to blossom and bear much fruit.

> *The wilderness and the solitary place shall be glad for them; and the desert shall rejoice, and blossom as the rose.*
> *It shall blossom abundantly, and rejoice even with joy and singing: the glory of Lebanon shall be given unto it, the excellency of Carmel and Sharon, they shall see the glory of the LORD, and the excellency of our God.*
> Isaiah 35:1-2. KJV

END NOTES:

[1] An old children's hymn, author unknown.

[2] Used by permission. For more information on the Fuller family and their music, you can visit their website at: www.fullerfamilyministries.com. I greatly appreciate the Fuller's beautiful gift of song writing and have included several of their songs in this book.

[3] "In the Garden" by C. Austin Miles. Verse 1.

[4] Ibid. Verse 2.

[5] Ibid. Verse 3.

[6] "Just As I Am" by Charlotte Elliott

[7] "Come, Ye Sinners, Poor and Needy" by Joseph Hart

[8] "Come, Ye Sinners, Poor and Needy" by Joseph Hart

[9] Psalm 103:12.

[10] "Nothing But the Blood" by Robert Lowry

[11] Used by permission.

[12] Taken from Enjoying Intimacy With God. Original edition ©1980 by The Moody Bible Institute of Chicago. This edition ©2000 by Discovery House Publishers and used by permission of Discovery House Publishers, Grand Rapids, MI 49501. All rights reserved.

[13] Ibid., pg. 23.

[14] Ibid., pg. 25-26.

[15] Ibid., pg. 27.

[16] American Dictionary of the English Language, Noah Webster, 1828. Reprinted by the Foundation for American Christian Education, San Francisco, CA, 1995.

[17] "The Green Pastures of Home" by Teresa Nuckols.

[18] This poem was found in a collection of poetry from an elderly lady, Ruby England, whom I met while working as a recreation leader at a local nursing home. Though I have searched for the author, I haven't been able to find out who wrote this lovely poem.

[19] Streams in the Desert Volume 1, Mrs. Charles E. Cowman, Zondervan Publishing House, 1965, pages 325-326.